Madness

A Brief History

Madness

A Brief History

Roy Porter

OXFORD
UNIVERSITY PRESS

OXFORD
UNIVERSITY PRESS

Great Clarendon Street, Oxford OX2 6DP

Oxford University Press is a department of the University of Oxford.
It furthers the University's objective of excellence in research, scholarship,
and education by publishing worldwide in

Oxford New York

Auckland Bangkok Buenos Aires Cape Town Chennai
Dar es Salaam Delhi Hong Kong Istanbul Karachi Kolkata
Kuala Lumpur Madrid Melbourne Mexico City Mumbai Nairobi
São Paulo Shanghai Singapore Taipei Tokyo Toronto

and an associated company in Berlin

Oxford is a registered trade mark of Oxford University Press
in the UK and in certain other countries

Published in the United States
by Oxford University Press Inc., New York

British Library Cataloguing in Publication Data

Data available
Library of Congress Cataloging in Publication Data

Porter, Roy, 1946– .
Madness: a brief history/Roy Porter.
Includes bibliographical references and index.
1. Mental illness—History. 2. Mentally ill—Care—History. 3. Psychiatry—History. I. Title.
[DNLM: 1. Mental Disorders—history. 2. Psychiatry—history. WM 11.1 P847m2002]
RC438.P67 2002 616.89′009—dc21 2001052329

ISBN 0–19–280266–6

1 3 5 7 9 10 8 6 4 2

Typeset in New Baskerville
by RefineCatch Limited, Bungay, Suffolk
Printed in Spain by
Book Print S.L., Barcelona

Acknowledgements

My thanks to Katharine Reeve of Oxford University Press, who first suggested this book and who has been supportive and critically constructive throughout. Over the last few months, successive drafts have been read by Hal Cook, Emese Lafferton, Chandak Sengoopta, Desirée Cox-Maksimov, and Natsu Hattori, for whose perceptive comments and candid criticism I am deeply grateful. Drawing upon the marvellous resources of the Iconographical Collection of the Wellcome Trust Library for the History and Understanding of Medicine, Andrea Meyer-Ludowisy has carried out the picture research with the blend of imagination and efficiency which makes her unique.

I am delighted to acknowledge the enormous support given to me by members of the staff of the Wellcome Trust Centre, notably my secretaries, first Rebecca Baker and then Emma Ford; retyping of numerous drafts has been done by the tireless and unfailing Sheila Lawler. Thanks also to Jed Lawler for coming to the rescue of a computer illiterate. My thanks also to Mary Worthington, who proved an excellent copy-editor, and finally to Jane Henderson for the index.

Contents

List of illustrations

The illustrations are reproduced by kind permission of the Wellcome Trust Library for the History and Understanding of Medicine.

1

Introduction

To 'define true madness'—the speaker is Polonius, labouring, as ever, to be wittily wise—'what is't but to be nothing else but mad?' Shakespeare's greybeard pedant hit the nail on the head this time: isn't insanity the mystery of mysteries? Even professors of psychiatry hold the most surprising views on the subject they profess. In a brace of books, *The Myth of Mental Illness* (1961) and *The Manufacture of Madness* (1970), Thomas Szasz, Professor of Psychiatry at Syracuse University (New York), denied there was any such thing as 'mental illness': it was not a fact of nature but a man-made 'myth'. He explained further:

> Psychiatry is conventionally defined as a medical speciality concerned with the diagnosis and treatment of mental diseases. I submit that this definition, which is still widely accepted, places psychiatry in the company of alchemy and astrology and commits it to the category of pseudoscience.

Why so? The reason was plain: 'there is no such thing as "mental illness" '.

For Szasz, who has continued to uphold these opinions for the last forty years, mental illness is not a disease, whose nature is being elucidated by science; it is rather a myth, fabricated by psychiatrists for reasons of professional advancement and endorsed by society because it sanctions easy solutions for problem people. Over the centuries, he alleges, medical men and their supporters have been involved in a self-serving 'manufacture of madness', by affixing psychiatric labels to people who are social pests, odd, or challenging. And in this orgy of stigmatization, organic psychiatrists have been no less to blame than Freud and his followers, whose invention of the Unconscious (Szasz alleges) breathed new life into defunct metaphysics of the mind and theologies of the soul.

All expectation of finding the aetiology of mental illness in body or mind—not to mention some Freudian underworld—is, in Szasz's view, a category mistake or sheer bad faith: 'mental illness' and the 'unconscious' are but metaphors, and misleading ones at that. In reifying such loose talk, psychiatrists have either naively pictorialized the psyche or been complicit in shady professional imperialism, pretending to expertise they do not possess. In view of all this, standard approaches to insanity and its history are vitiated by hosts of illicit assumptions and *questions mal posées*.

Szasz has not been alone. *Madness and Civilization*, which appeared in French in 1961, the work of the Paris historian of thought Michel Foucault, similarly argued that mental illness must be understood not as a natural fact but as a cultural construct, sustained by a grid of administrative and medico-psychiatric practices. The history of madness properly written would thus be an account not of disease and its treatment but of questions of freedom and control, knowledge and power.

Less radically, but equally unsettlingly, two highly respected British psychiatrists, Richard Hunter and Ida Macalpine, were pointing, around the same time, to the profound muddle which psychiatry had got itself into:

> there is not even an objective method of describing or communicating clinical findings without subjective interpretation and no exact and uniform terminology which conveys precisely the same to all. In consequence there is wide divergence of diagnosis, even of diagnoses, a steady flow of new terms and an ever-changing nomenclature, as well as a surfeit of hypotheses which tend to be presented as fact. Furthermore, aetiology remains speculative, pathogenesis largely obscure, classifications predominantly symptomatic and hence

arbitrary and possibly ephemeral; physical treatments are empirical and subject to fashion, and psychotherapies still only in their infancy and doctrinaire.

Szasz's and Foucault's provocative formulations—which stand traditional progressive ('Whiggish') history of psychiatry on its head, recasting its heroes as villains—have in their turn been robustly rebutted. In *The Reality of Mental Illness* (1986), Martin Roth, Professor of Psychiatry at Cambridge University, and Jerome Kroll counter-argue that the stability of psychiatric symptoms over time shows that mental illness is no mere label or scapegoating device, but a real psychopathological entity, with an authentic organic basis.

These drastic splits within psychiatry as to the nature of mental illness (reality, convention, or illusion?) show how wise old Polonius was. And, following his wisdom, the brief historical survey which follows makes no attempt to define true madness or fathom the *nature* of mental illness; it rests content with a brief, bold, and unbiased account of its *history*. Yet psychiatry's past, as well as its scientific status, has also been hotly contested. 'The story in its broad outlines is familiar', wrote Sir Aubrey Lewis, the eminent director of the Institute of Psychiatry, attached to the Maudsley Hospital in London, in a review of Foucault's book:

After the tortures and judicial murders of the Middle Ages and the Renaissance, which confounded demoniacal possession with delusion and frenzy, and smelt out witchcraft in the maunderings of demented old women, there were the cruelties and degradation of the madhouses of the seventeenth and eighteenth centuries, in which authority used chains and whips as its instruments. Humanitarian effort put an end to the abuses. Pinel in France, Chiarugi in Italy, Tuke in England inaugurated an era of kindness and medical care, which prepared the way for a rational, humane approach to the mastery of mental illness. In the nineteenth century the pathology of insanity was investigated, its clinical forms described and classified, its kinship with physical disease and the psychoneuroses recognized. Treatment was undertaken in university hospitals, out-patient clinics multiplied, social aspects were given increasing attention. By the end of the century the way had been opened for the ideas of such men as Kraepelin, Freud, Charcot and Janet, following in the paths of Kahlbaum and Griesinger, Conolly and Maudsley. In the twentieth century psychopathology has been elucidated, and psychological treatment given ever widening scope and sanction. Revolutionary changes have occurred in physical methods of treatment, the regime in mental hospitals has been further liberalized, and the varieties of care articulated into one another, individualized, and made elements in a continuous therapeutic process

2ᵉ. Epreuve de l'Eau froide

1 The cold-water ordeal is depicted in this seventeenth-century French print: a man is tortured by being tied with rope and lowered into cold water. Violent immersion in cold water was a form of divine ordeal, often used on witches: if they floated they were guilty, if they sank, they were innocent. It was also a supposed cure for madness.

that extends well into the general community, beginning with the phase of onset, *stadium incrementi*, and proceeding to the ultimate phase of rehabilitation and social resettlement.

'This', concluded Lewis, 'is the conventional picture, one of progress and enlightenment . . . it is not far out.'

Or is it? Over the past generation, the history of psychiatry as set out by the accounts digested by Lewis has been denied, and controversy has raged as to how to interpret many crucial developments: the rise and fall of the asylum ('a convenient place for inconvenient people'?); the politics of compulsory confinement and then of 'decarceration'; the origins, scientific status, and therapeutic claims of psychoanalysis (was Freud a fraud?); the 'beneficence' of the psychiatric profession; the justification of such questionable treatments as clitoridectomy, frontal lobotomy, and electroconvulsive therapy; and the role played by psychiatry in the socio-sexual control of ethnic minorities, women, and gay people, and other social 'victims'—to name just a few. The last thirty years have brought a ferment of original scholarship—often passionate, partisan, and polemical—in all these areas and many more, which shows no signs of abating. Building upon such studies, this book will assess what credibility mainstream views as summarized by Lewis still possess.

A bill of fare might be helpful. The next chapter looks at madness understood as divine or demonic possession. Prevalent amongst pre-literate peoples the world over, such supernatural beliefs were then embodied in Mesopotamian and Egyptian medicine and in Greek myth and art. As reformulated and authorized by the teachings of Christianity, they remained current in the West till the eighteenth century, though increasingly discounted by medicine and science.

It is to the birth of medical science that Chapter 3 turns, examining the rational and naturalistic thinking about madness developed by Graeco-Roman philosophers and doctors and incorporated in the subsequent Western medical tradition. Lunacy and folly meanwhile became symbolically charged in art and literature: these cultural motifs and meanings of madness are explored in Chapter 4. Taking madness in society, Chapter 5 proceeds to examine the drive to institutionalize the insane which peaked in the mid-twentieth century, when half a million people were psychiatrically detained in the USA and some 150,000 in the UK.

The 'new science' of the seventeenth century replaced Greek thinking with new models of body, brain, and disease: the early psychiatric theories and practices which derived from them form the core of Chapter 6. And the following chapter turns to psychiatry's subjects: what did the insane themselves think and feel? How did they regard the treatment they received, so often against their will?

The twentieth century has been widely called the 'psychiatric century', and so a whole chapter (Chapter 8) is given over to its developments. Particular attention is given to one of its great innovations, the rise (and fall?) of psychoanalysis, and also to major innovations in treatments via surgery and drugs. Psychiatry's standing as science and therapy at the dawn of the twenty-first century is then briefly assessed in the Conclusion: has its chequered history anything to tell us about the psychiatric enterprise at large?

As will be evident, much is omitted. There is nothing on non-Western ideas of insanity or psychiatry. I have not engaged with questions of social psychopathology (what makes people go mad in the first place?), nor have I tried to explore the representations of madness in high culture or the popular media. In such a short book, I have focused on a few core questions: who has been identified as mad? What has been thought to cause their condition? And, what action has been taken to cure or secure them?

2

Gods and demons

Those whom the gods destroy, they first make mad.
(Euripides)

In the beginning

Madness may be as old as mankind. Archaeologists have unearthed skulls datable back to at least 5000 BC which have been trephined or trepanned—small round holes have been bored in them with flint tools. The subject was probably thought to be possessed by devils which the holes would allow to escape.

Madness figures, usually as a fate or punishment, in early religious myths and in heroic fables. In Deuteronomy (6: 5) it is written, 'The Lord will smite thee with madness'; the Old Testament tells of many possessed of devils, and relates how the Lord punished Nebuchadnezzar by reducing him to bestial madness. Homer has

2 In the Old Testament Nebuchadnezzar, king of Babylon, has a dream, which Daniel interprets as a harbinger of madness. When he later spoke with pride of how he had built his wonderful palace, God's voice announces that 'the Kingdom is departed from thee', and Nebuchadnezzar is driven mad, as in the dream.

mad Ajax slaughtering sheep in the deranged belief that they were enemy soldiers, a scene presaging Cervantes' Don Quixote tilting at windmills. Violence, grief, blood-lust, and cannibalism have commonly been associated with insanity. Herodotus described the crazy King Cambyses of Persia mocking religion—who but a madman would dishonour the gods?

Wild disturbances of mood, speech, and behaviour were generally imputed to supernatural powers. Hindu-ism has a special demon, Grahi ('she who seizes'), who is held responsible for epileptic convulsions, while in India a dog-demon is also accused of seizing the suf-ferer. (Canine traits and madness have often been linked, as in the widespread belief in werewolves—lycanthropy, or 'wolf-madness'—in which the madman prowls about graves and bays at the moon, or, in the use of the term 'the black dog' for depression.)

The Babylonians and Mesopotamians held that cer-tain disorders were caused by spirit invasion, sorcery, demonic malice, the evil eye, or the breaking of taboos; possession was both judgement and punishment. An Assyrian text of around 650 BC puts what were evidently epileptic symptoms down to devils:

> If at the time of his possession, while he is sitting down, his left eye moves to the side, a lip puckers, saliva flows

from his mouth, and his hand, leg and trunk on the left side jerk like a slaughtered sheep, it is *migtu*. If at the time of possession his mind is awake, the demon can be driven out; if at the time of his possession his mind is not so aware, the demon cannot be driven out.

Early Greek attitudes can be gathered from myths and epics. These do not present faculties like reason and will in the manner familiar from later medicine and philosophy, neither do their heroes possess psyches comparable to that, say, of Sophocles' Oedipus, still less to those found in Shakespeare or Freud. Homeric man was not the introspective self-conscious being who populates Socrates' dialogues a few hundred years later—indeed, *The Iliad* has no word for 'person' or 'oneself'. Living and conduct, normal and abnormal alike, were rather seen as being at the mercy of external, supernatural forces, and humans are portrayed as literally driven to distraction with wrath, anguish, or vengefulness. *The Iliad*'s protagonists are puppets, in the grip of terrible forces beyond their control—gods, demons, and the Furies—which punish, avenge, and destroy: and their fates are decided largely by decree from above, as is sometimes revealed through dreams, oracles, and divination. The inner life, with its agonizing dilemmas of conscience and choice, has not yet become decisive, and we hear far more about heroes' deeds than their deliberations.

A more modern mental landscape was emerging, however, by the time of Athens's golden age. The thinking on the psyche developed in the fifth and fourth centuries BC set the mould for mainstream reasoning about minds and madness in the West, as was tacitly acknowledged by Freud when he named infantile psycho-sexual conflicts the 'Oedipus Complex', paying tribute to Sophocles' play. Greek drama combines elements of both traditional and of newer casts of mind.

The plays of Aeschylus, Sophocles, and Euripides dramatize terrible elemental conflicts—a hero or heroine tormented as a plaything of the gods or crushed under ineluctable destiny, the rival demands of love and honour, of duty and desire, of individual, kin, and state. Sometimes the inescapable result is madness: they go out of their minds, raging and rampaging utterly out of control, as when Medea slays her children. Unlike Homer's heroes, however, the tragedians' protagonists are the *conscious* subjects of reflection, responsibility, and guilt; they betray inner conflict as agonized minds divided against themselves, as is often echoed in the contradictory thinking-out-loud of the Chorus. The powers of destruction in the tragedies are no longer solely those of external fate, proud gods, and malevolent furies. Ruin is also self-inflicted—heroes are consumed with hubris, with ambition or pride, followed by shame, grief, and guilt; they tear themselves apart, and help to bring their own madness upon themselves (nemesis): psychic civil war becomes endemic to the human condition.

Drama also suggested paths to resolution—or, as we might say, theatre served as 'therapy'. Transgression might, of course, simply be punished in death. But, as with Oedipus, agony was shown as the path to a higher wisdom; blindness could lead to insight, and the public enactment of drama itself could provide a collective catharsis (purging). Shakespeare would show the same happening with King Lear, whose self-alienation led at last, via madness, to self-knowledge.

The supernatural beliefs about possession typical of the archaic age were also confronted and challenged by Greek medicine. As already noted, the gods had traditionally been held responsible for epileptic fits, the victim of the 'sacred disease' being overcome by a demon or spirit which wrestled with his body and soul. The disorder was in turn countered by prayers, incantations, and sacrifices offered at temples dedicated to Asklepios, the god of healing.

A treatise 'On the Sacred Disease' demurred. Its author, a follower of the so-called 'father of Greek medicine', Hippocrates (*c.*460–357 BC), could not find anything supernatural in the condition. Epilepsy was simply a disease of the brain:

> the sacred disease appears to me to be no more divine nor more sacred than other diseases, but has a natural cause from which it originates like other afflictions. Men regard its nature and cause as divine from ignorance and wonder, because it is not like other diseases.

The Hippocratic author catalogued with sneering delight the different gods supposed to bring about the distinctive forms of seizure. If the sufferer behaved in a goat-like way, or ground his teeth, or if the right side were convulsed, Hera, the mother of the gods, was blamed. If the patient kicked and foamed at the mouth, Ares was responsible. And so forth. Call it sacred merely because of its bizarre symptoms, and you would have to do the same with no end of illnesses. With the example of epilepsy in mind, Hippocratic medicine naturalized madness, and so brought it down from the gods. The explanatory theories it developed will be explored in the following chapter.

Christian madness

The Emperor Constantine recognized Christianity in the Roman Empire in AD 313, and the subsequent triumph of the Church and conversion of the barbarian invaders gave official sanction in the centuries to come for supernatural thinking about insanity. Unlike Greek philosophy, Christianity denied that reason was the essence of man: what counted were sin, divine will, and love, and a believer's faith (*credo quia absurdum*: I believe because it is absurd). It preached, moreover, an apocalyptic narrative of sin and redemption in which the human race was vastly outnumbered by otherworldly spiritual beings—God and His angels and saints, the souls of the departed, Satan and all his squadrons—to say nothing of the ghosts, wood-demons, and hobgoblins omnipresent in peasant lore and semi-sanctioned by the Church's supernaturalism. (Folk beliefs in traditional societies typically view some diseases as supernatural, and hence in need of magical remedies. Pulverized human skull was widely recommended, for instance, for the treatment of epilepsy.)

In Christian divinity, the Holy Ghost and the Devil battled for possession of the individual soul. The marks of such 'psychomachy' might include despair, anguish, and other symptoms of disturbance of mind. The

3 A seventeenth-century epileptic being restrained by another man is brought before a priest to be blessed. Epilepsy was long associated with the supernatural and hence the Church was involved in its treatment.

Church also entertained a madness which was holy, patterned upon the 'madness of the Cross' (the scandal of Christ crucified) and exhibited in the ecstatic revelations of saints and mystics. Holy innocents, prophets, ascetics, and visionaries too might be possessed by a 'good madness'. But derangement was more commonly viewed as diabolic, schemed by Satan and spread by witches and heretics. In his *Anatomy of Melancholy* (1621), the Oxford don Robert Burton thus identified the Tempter as the true author of despair and suicide, if often working through such victims as the sick whose weaknesses made them particularly susceptible. His contemporary, the Anglican clergyman Richard Napier, who doubled as a doctor and specialized in healing those 'unquiet of mind', found that many who consulted him were suffering from religious despair, the dread of damnation aroused by Calvinist Puritanism, the seductions of Satan, or fear of bewitchment.

Unclean spirits were to be treated by spiritual means: amongst Catholics, the performance of masses, exorcism, or pilgrimage to a shrine, like that at Gheel in the Netherlands, where Saint Dymphna exercised singular healing powers. The insane were also cared for in religious houses. Protestants like Napier preferred prayer, Bible-reading, and counsel.

The witch craze which gathered momentum across

4 In this seventeenth-century biblical scene of Christ healing the sick, the dishevelled woman in the foreground is holding her hands to her eyes in a gesture of madness.

Europe from the late fifteenth century, peaking around 1650, likewise viewed uncontrolled speech and behaviour as symptoms of satanic *maleficium* (malice) directed by witches who had compacted with the Devil. In the conflagration of heresy-accusations and burnings stoked by the Reformation and Counter-Reformation, false doctrine and delusion formed two sides of the same coin: the mad were judged to be possessed, and religious adversaries were deemed out of their mind.

'I was seiz'd with great Fear and Trembling'

Believers themselves personally experienced madness and despair as indications of sin, diabolical possession, or a lost soul. A high proportion of the autobiographical writings of mad people (see for example Margery Kempe and John Perceval, discussed below in Chapter 7) have been religious.

Born in Exeter in 1631 into a wealthy family of Anglican lawyers, George Trosse later looked back at his youth as a Sodom of sin—turning into a 'very Atheist', he had followed every 'cursed, carnal principle' which had fired his lusts.

Pricked by a 'roving Fancy, a Desire to get Riches, and to live luxuriously in the World', as he recorded in his autobiography, Trosse travelled abroad to enjoy the 'unregenerate World; the Lusts of the Flesh, the Lusts of the Eyes, and the Pride of Life', being led into 'great Sins and dangerous Snares', and indulging in 'the most abominable Uncleannesses' short of 'compleat Acts of Fornication'. Even grave illness did not lead him to think on death and damnation, or on the merciful Providence which had spared him.

Eventually he returned home, a notorious sinner against all the Commandments, enslaved to a licentiousness which had hardened his heart. Crisis ensued. After one particularly gross drinking bout, he awoke hearing 'some rushing kind of noise' and seeing a 'shadow' at the foot of his bed. 'I was seiz'd with great Fear and Trembling', Trosse recalled. A voice demanded: 'Who art thou?' Convinced it must be God, he contritely replied, 'I am a very great Sinner, Lord!', and fell to his knees and prayed. The voice proceeded: 'Yet more humble; yet more humble.' He removed his stockings, to pray upon his bare knees. The voice continued. He pulled off his hose and doublet. Warned he still was not low enough, he found a hole in the floor and crept within, praying while covering himself in dirt.

The voice then commanded him to cut off his hair, and at this point he anticipated it would next tell him to slit his throat. Spiritual illumination now dawned: the voice was not God's but the Devil's! Knowing he had 'greatly offended', he finally heard a call: 'Thou Wretch! Thou has committed the Sin against the Holy Ghost.' Falling into despair—the sin against the Holy Ghost which was reputed to be unpardonable—he wanted to curse God and die, and his head exploded with a babel of clamouring voices, making a 'Torment of my Conscience'.

Buffeted by further voices and visions, Trosse fell into a 'distracted condition'. His friends, fortunately, knew of a physician of Glastonbury in Somerset who was 'esteem'd very skilful and successful in such cases'. There they carried him by main force, strapped to a horse; he resisted with all his might, believing he was being dragged down into the 'regions of hell'. Voices taunted: 'What, must he go yet farther into hell? O fearful, O dreadful!' The Devil, Trosse later recalled, had taken complete possession.

He identified the Glastonbury madhouse with hell, seeing its fetters as satanic torments and his fellow patients as 'executioners'. Eventually, however, though long seeking 'revenge and rebellion' against God, he grew more tranquil, largely thanks to the doctor's wife, 'a very religious woman', who would pray with him, until his 'blasphemies' began to subside. Finally 'I bewail'd my sins', and he was thought to have recovered enough to return to Exeter.

Alas! Like the proverbial dog to his vomit, he returned to his old ways. This time, however, the fight with the Tempter was in the open. He now applied to godly ministers for guidance in removing his 'great load of guilt'. Carried once again to Glastonbury, he 'rag'd against God', believing that he had sinned once more against the Holy Ghost, but the doctor 'reduc'd [me] again to a Composedness and Calmness of Mind'.

Even then, his regeneration was not complete, for his faith was but 'Pharisaical'. Backsliding, he was induced to return for a third time to Glastonbury. Finally, and this time permanently, 'God was pleas'd, after all my repeated Provocations, to restore me to Peace and Serenity, and the regular Use of my Reason'. A man reborn, Trosse went off to study at Oxford. With divine assistance, he was called to the ministry, and he became a pious Nonconformist preacher.

The Trosse who then penned his autobiography—a conversion narrative comparable to Bunyan's *Grace Abounding*—had a well-defined religious concept of madness. Reason was walking in harmony with God, derangement that state of mind when the soul, diabolically assailed, blasphemed against the Almighty. Madness was thus a desperate, acute phase in the trial and redemption of souls, because it brought a sinner into a state of crisis, and provided the prelude to recovery.

Against the grain

The bloody excesses of witch- and heresy-hunting— over 200,000 people, mainly women, were executed during the witch craze—eventually bred official and public scepticism about demoniacal possession. An early medical expression of this doubt is contained in the *De Praestigiis Daemonum* [On the Conjuring Tricks of Demons: 1563] of Johannes Weyer, a medical officer from Arnhem in the Netherlands. Weyer warned how readily illness in the old, the solitary, the ignorant, could be mistaken for witchcraft. The Fiend could indeed influence human behaviour, Weyer conceded, but since his power was ultimately limited by God, those he was capable of afflicting were melancholics and others prone to disturbances of the imagination. Witches fantasized the enormities which they confessed, and their imaginings were the products of hallucinatory drugs or dreams. Likewise, the crimes of which they were accused—inflicting sudden death, impotence, crop failure, and other misfortunes—were purely natural disasters. Supposed witches were to be pitied and treated, not feared and punished.

Reginald Scot from Kent, author of the *Discovery of Witchcraft* (1584), trod in Weyer's footsteps and similarly questioned the reality of witchcraft—it was chiefly to refute his scepticism that King James, an orthodox Scottish Presbyterian, wrote his *Daemonologie* (1597). From around that time Anglican leaders questioned supposed instances of demonic possession, fearing that such sensations played into the hands of Papists and Puritans: their manifestations were put down instead to fraud or the self-deluding fancies of zealots and the vulgar. For the same reasons the Anglican Church ceased to make use of exorcism.

Physicians too expressed their doubts—not generally about the *possibility* of supernaturally induced madness as such but about its *proof* in the particular instance. With three other London doctors, Edward Jorden was summoned in 1603 to testify in the case of Elizabeth Jackson, arraigned on a charge of bewitching the 14-year-old Mary Glover. The latter had begun to suffer from 'fittes . . . so fearfull, that all that were about her, supposed that she would dye'; she had become speechless and temporarily blind, and her left side was anaesthetized and paralysed. Classic symptoms: but was it *maleficium* or sickness?

Glover had first been treated by physicians from the Royal College, but when she failed to respond, they deemed, perhaps all too predictably, that there was something 'beyond naturall' in it. Jorden demurred, however, arguing for disease, and he defended his medical explanation in a book whose title staked his claims: *A Briefe Discourse of a Disease Called the Suffocation of the Mother. Written uppon occasion which hath beene of late taken thereby, to suspect possession of an evill spirit, or some such like supernaturall power. Wherein is declared that divers strange actions and passions of the body of man, which in the common opinion are imputed to the Divill, have their true naturall causes, and do accompany this disease* (1603). Jorden named Glover's condition the 'suffocation of the mother' (i.e., matrix or womb), or simply the 'mother': that is, 'hysteria'. Such symptoms as digestive blockages and feelings of suffocation pointed to a uterine pathology. Relying on Galen's teachings, he argued that irregularities of the womb bred 'vapours' which wafted through the body, inducing physical disorders in the extremities, the abdomen, and even the brain, thereby producing the paroxysms, convulsive dancing, etc., so often misattributed to possession, yet properly explained by 'the suffocation of the mother'. Jorden's prime concern was to establish a *natural* explanation.

Medical interventions like Jorden's could exonerate

a woman from being judged the Devil's disciple, and her life might thus be spared. Its downside might then be to draw down on her the charge of being guilty of 'imposture'—being a fake witch. In later centuries, 'hysterical' women were stigmatized much as 'witches' had been, though they escaped legal penalties: misogyny remained, only the diagnosis changed. In a revealing letter to his friend Wilhelm Fliess, Freud noted how he could understand the witch-hunters of bygone times.

Enlightened opinions

Opinions like Scot's and Jorden's were to find increasingly receptive ears among educated elites. The Thirty Years War (1618–48) on the Continent and the Civil Wars in Britain (1642–51) stirred strong reactions against religio-political extremism, condemned as ruinous to public order and personal safety alike.

A barrage of invective was unleashed against Anabaptists, Ranters, Antinomians (those who believed that the Holy Spirit resided within them and that 'to the pure all things are pure'), and other self-styled saints who assailed public order in church and state alike. Their anarchic teachings were denounced not just on grounds scriptural, theological, and demonological, but *medical* too: these puffed-up prophets were literally brain-sick, 'inspired' not with the Holy Spirit but with wind.

Doctors and their allies pointed to the affinities between the religious fringe and outright lunatics: did not both display glossolalia (speaking in tongues), convulsions, weepings and wailings, and similar symptoms? 'Enthusiasm' was read as a sign of psychopathology. Some likened 'zeal' to epilepsy; a surfeit of black bile was blamed by humoralist doctors; while the new mechanical philosophy suggested that religious swoonings and spasms could be inflicted by inflamed fibres, vascular obstructions, or smoky vapours ascending into the head from obstructed guts and clouding the judgement. On such grounds Thomas Willis—seventeenth-century Anglican, royalist, and coiner of the term 'neurologie'—thus excluded the Devil: so-called possession was all a matter of defects of the nerves and brain. Especially after 1650, elites thus washed their hands of witchcraft: it was not a Satanic plot but individual sickness or collective hysteria; eighteenth-century magistrates similarly deemed converts who shrieked and swooned at Methodist meetings fit for Bedlam—John Wesley himself, by contrast, upheld belief both in witchcraft and in demonic possession.

In England, as late as the 1630s, a physician as distinguished as Sir Thomas Browne might give evidence
in court backing the reality of witchcraft. In other parts
of Europe, the demonological debates rumbled on
longer. Around 1700, Friedrich Hoffmann, the great
medical professor at Halle in Prussia, was at the thick of
attempts to resolve that issue in the German-speaking
lands. In Jena in 1693 a Dr Ernst Heinrich Wedel
advanced the claim that 'spectres are fictitious representations, against the law of nature'. Hoffmann for his
part stated that the Devil acted upon witches through
the animal spirits, and one of his students reaffirmed
the Devil's influence over both the mind and the body.

In the Dutch Republic, France, and Britain, all prominent physicians by Hoffmann's time explained
religious melancholy wholly naturalistically. Referring
to the visions of Quakers and other sectaries, Dr
Nicholas Robinson, an avid Newtonian, claimed they
were mere madness, and arose from the 'stronger
impulses of a warm brain'. Dr Richard Mead's *Medica
Sacra* (1749) provided rational explanations for possession and other diseases traditionally credited to the
Devil: such beliefs were 'vulgar errors . . . the bugbears
of children and women'.

A generation later the Midlands practitioner and
champion of enlightened thought Erasmus Darwin was

aghast at the survival of popular belief in the workings of Satan. In his *Zoonomia* (1794) and elsewhere, he blamed the Wesleyans for preaching hellfire and damnation: 'Many theatric preachers among the Methodists successfully inspire this terror, and live comfortably upon the folly of their hearers. In this kind of madness the poor patients frequently commit suicide.' Himself an unbeliever, Darwin cited case histories of wretched sufferers whose 'scruples' had plunged them into religious madness, and thence to despair and death:

> Mr —, a clergyman, formerly of this neighbourhood, began to bruise and wound himself for the sake of religious mortification . . . As he had a wife and family of small children, I believed the case to be incurable; as otherwise the affection and employment in his family connections would have opposed the beginning of this insanity. He was taken to a madhouse without effect, and after he returned home, continued to beat and bruise himself, and by this kind of mortification, and by sometimes long fasting, he at length became emaciated and died . . . what cruelties, murders, massacres, has not this insanity introduced into the world.

Thus religious madness—indeed all belief in the existence of supernatural intervention in human affairs—was turned into a matter of psychopathology.

Secularizing madness

The witch-hunts resulted from a marriage of traditional popular belief in the supernatural with the learned demonology advanced by Protestant and Counter-Reformation theology, Renaissance magic, and renewed anti-heresy crusades. From the mid-seventeenth century the ruling orders were giving such teachings up: not only did they seem irrational and pre-scientific, but they had failed to provide guarantees for social order. Witches ceased to be prosecuted and began to be patronized—though it was a case of 'new witches for old', with the new scapegoats including beggars, criminals, and vagrants. John Locke wrote to insist upon *The Reasonableness of Christianity* (1694): even religion now had to be rational.

This pathologization of religious madness led Enlightenment free-thinkers to pathologize religiosity at large. In effect, this was also, much later, Freud's position. God was an illusion, faith 'wish-fulfilment', and belief, though all too real, was a mental projection satisfying neurotic needs, to be explained in terms of the sublimation of suppressed sexuality or of the death wish. In reducing religion to psychopathology, Freud was echoing the more biting of the *philosophes*, like Voltaire and Diderot, who adjudged Christian beliefs the morbid secretion of sick brains.

These days, while the Churches continue to accept, in principle, the reality of visions, spirit possession, and exorcism, they are profoundly suspicious of credulity and deception. The Roman Catholic or Anglican who claims to be assailed by the Devil has become an embarrassment. His priest may try to persuade him that such doctrines are merely metaphorical; and, if he persists, he may be urged to see a psychotherapist.

As just shown, opposition to religious models of madness was largely expressed through the concepts and language of medicine. In time doctors replaced clergy in handling the insane. It is to medical theories of abnormal thought and behaviour that we now turn.

Madness rationalized

'The *original* or *primary* cause of Madness is a mystery'
(William Pargeter, 1792)

Reasoning about madness

Early civilizations, as we have seen, saw madness as
supernaturally inflicted. The Assyrians and Egyptians
regarded many diseases as hurled from the heavens;
healing was therefore entrusted to priest-doctors, and
for diagnostic and therapeutic purposes they had
recourse to auguries, sacrifice, and divination. Archaic
Greek myths and epics similarly viewed madness as a
visitation from the gods, while popular lore ascribed
illnesses to spirits, and hoped to restore health through
divine intercession at Aesculapian shrines.

The philosophers who emerged in the Greek-
speaking city-states from the sixth century BC onwards,

however, viewed the cosmos and the human condition naturalistically. Socrates notoriously slighted the gods and, with his pupil Plato, analysed the psyche's constituents: reason, spirit, the passions, and the soul. In due course Aristotle, Plato's pupil, defined man as a rational animal, within the system of Nature. Man, for Protagoras, was the measure of all things.

The Greek philosophies of the fifth and fourth centuries BC systematically reasoned about nature, society, and consciousness, in attempts to fathom the order of things. Thinkers cast the rational individual—or, more precisely, educated, eminent males like themselves—as the paradigm for ethical and political ideals. In thus championing reason, they did not deny the reality of the irrational. On the contrary, the great store they set by rational thought and action attests what dangers they saw in the passions and in the blind destructive force of fate: only the calm pursuit of reason could rescue humans from catastrophe.

Plato (*c.*428–*c.*348 BC) in particular condemned appetite as the arch-enemy of human freedom and dignity; and the Platonic polarization of the rational and the irrational, enshrining as it did the superiority of mind over matter, became definitive of Classical values in such later philosophies as Stoicism, expounded by Seneca, Cicero, and Marcus Aurelius.

Through self-knowledge—the Delphic oracle's 'know thyself'—reason could analyse and explain human nature and thereby master enslaving appetites. Terrified by the titanic and primordial forces disrupting the mind, Platonism, Pythagoreanism, Stoicism, and similar schools of philosophy exposed the irrational as a danger and disgrace which reason or the soul must combat.

By exalting *mind* and valuing order and logic, Greek thinkers defined for future ages—even if they did not solve!—the problem of the irrational. In making man the measure of all things, they plucked madness from the heavens and humanized it. They also adduced various schemes for explaining disorders of the mind. So how did the Greeks account for that shipwreck of the soul—and hope to prevent or cure it?

Medicalizing madness

Complementing the theatrical and philosophical traditions already noted was medicine. Above all, in those texts known as the Hippocratic corpus, purportedly the teachings of Hippocrates of Cos, though in fact rather later, dating largely from the fourth century BC, Greek medicine developed a comprehensive holistic explanatory scheme for health and sickness within which madness was included. Hippocratic medicine aimed to aid Nature in creating and preserving a healthy mind in a healthy body.

Human life, in sickness and in health, was to be understood in naturalistic terms. As one of those Hippocratic texts tells us,

> Men ought to know that from the brain, and from the brain only, arise our pleasures, joys, laughter, and jests, as well as our sorrows, pains, griefs and tears. Through it, in particular, we think, see, hear, and distinguish the ugly from the beautiful, the bad from the good, the pleasant from the unpleasant. . . . It is the same thing which makes us mad or delirious, inspires us with dread and fear, whether by night or by day, brings sleeplessness, inopportune mistakes, aimless anxieties, absent-mindedness, and acts that are contrary to habit.

Medicine thus excluded the supernatural by definition.

Hippocratic medicine explained health and illness in terms of 'humours' (basic juices or fluids). The body was subject to rhythms of development and change, determined by the key humours constrained within the skin-envelope; health or illness resulted from their shifting balance. These crucial vitality-sustaining juices were blood, choler (or yellow bile), phlegm, and melancholy. They served distinct life-sustaining ends. Blood was the source of vitality. Choler or bile was the gastric juice, indispensable for digestion. Phlegm, a broad category comprehending all colourless secretions, was a lubricant and coolant. Visible in substances like sweat and tears, it was most evident when in excess—at times of cold and fever, when it appeared through the mouth and nose. The fourth fluid, black bile, or melancholy, seems more problematic. A dark liquid almost never found pure, it was reckoned responsible for darkening other fluids, as when blood, skin, or stools turned blackish. It was also the cause of dark hair, eyes, or skin pigmentation. Among them, the four major fluids accounted for the visible and tangible phenomena of physical existence: temperature, colour, and texture. Blood made the flesh hot and wet, choler hot and dry, phlegm cold and wet, and black bile produced cold and dry sensations.

Parallels were drawn with what Aristotle's philosophy called the 'elements' of the universe at large: air, fire, water, earth. Being warm, moist, and animated, blood was like air, while choler was like fire, being warm and dry; phlegm suggested water (cold and wet), and black bile (melancholy) resembled earth (cold and dry). Such analogies further pointed to and meshed with other facets of the natural world, central to Greek science, such as astrological influences and the cycles of

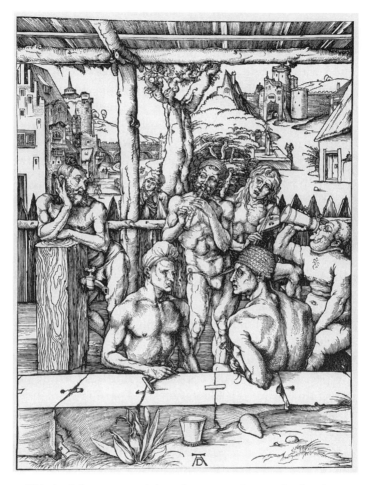

5 This bath-house containing six men and an onlooker is an allegory of the four humours and five senses; after Dürer, *c.*1496.

the seasons. Being cold and wet, winter thus had affinities with phlegm; it was the time people caught chills. Each fluid also had its distinctive colour—blood being red, choler yellow, phlegm pale, and melancholy dark. These hues were responsible for body coloration, explaining why particular races were white, black, red, or yellow, and why certain individuals were paler, swarthier, or ruddier than others.

Humoral balance also explained the temperaments, or what would, in later centuries, be called personality and psychological dispositions. Thus someone generously endowed with blood would present a florid complexion and have a 'sanguine' temperament, being lively, energetic, and robust, though perhaps given to hot-bloodedness and a short temper. Someone cursed with surplus choler or bile might be choleric or acrimonious, marked by an acid tongue. Likewise with phlegm (pale phlegmatic in character) and black bile (a person with swarthy appearance and a saturnine disposition, giving off 'black looks'). There was, in short, boundless explanatory potential in such rich holistic interlinkages of physiology, psychology, and bearing, not least because correspondences were suggested between inner constitutional states ('temper') and outer physical manifestations ('complexion'). Analogy-based explanatory systems of this kind were not just plausible but indispensable so long as science had little direct access to what went on beneath the skin or in the head. The values of Periclean Athens regarded the human body as noble, even sacred, and hence ruled out dissection.

Holistic in its disposition, humoral thinking had ready explanations for the plunge from health into illness, both physical and psychological (though in a holistic system, these were never polarized). All was well when the vital fluids cooperated in their proper balance. Illness resulted when one of them gathered (became 'plethoric') or dwindled. If, perhaps through faulty diet, the body made too much blood, 'sanguineous disorders' followed—in modern idiom, we might say that blood pressure rose—and one got overheated and feverish. One might, by consequence, have a seizure or apoplectic fit, or grow maniacal. Deficiency of blood or poor blood quality, by contrast, meant loss of vitality, while blood loss due to wounds would lead to fainting or death. Specifically in terms of mental disorder, excesses both of blood and of yellow bile could lead to mania, whereas a surplus of black bile—being too cold and dry—resulted in lowness, melancholy, or depression.

Fortunately such imbalances were capable of prevention or correction, through sensible lifestyle, or by medical or surgical means. The person whose liver 'concocted' a surfeit of blood or whose blood was polluted with toxins—both could cause mania—should undergo blood-letting (also known as phlebotomy or venesection), which was to enjoy a long future as the prophylactic and therapeutic sheet-anchor in Europe's lunatic asylums. A change of diet could help. Raving madmen would be put on a 'diluting' and 'cooling' diet, with salad greens, barley water, and milk, and a ban on wine and red meat. Enormously detailed recommendations were spelt out for the regulation of diet, exercise, and lifestyle.

Humoralism provided a comprehensive explanatory scheme, staking out bold archetypal parameters (hot/cold, wet/dry, etc.) and embracing the natural and the human, the physical and the psychological, the healthy and the pathological. Plain and commonsensical to the layman, it was also capable of technical elaboration by the physician.

Within humoralism's easy-to-visualize grid of opposites, it was simple to picture mental conditions as extensions of physical ones. In a scheme in which healthiness lay in equilibrium and sickness in extremes, mania implied—almost required—the presence of an equal but opposite pathological state: melancholy. The categories of mania and melancholy—representing hot and cold, wet and dry, 'red' and 'black' conditions respectively—became ingrained, intellectually, emotionally, and perhaps even aesthetically and subliminally, in the educated European mind, rather, perhaps, as key psychoanalytical concepts (repression, defence, projection, denial) did in the twentieth century.

The clinical gaze

Greek medicine did not develop this plausible and satisfying explanatory framework in the abstract: it was clinically grounded and full of practical applicability to the sick. Case histories from the Hippocratic writings onwards record mental abnormalities. In one, a woman is noted as being rambling in her speech and mouthing obscenities, exhibiting fears and depression and undergoing 'grief'; another woman, suffering anguish, 'without speaking a word . . . would fumble, pluck, scratch, pick hairs, weep and then laugh, but . . . not speak'. A case which reads like delusional melancholia, said to arise from black bile collecting in the liver and rising to the head, involved a condition which 'usually attacks abroad, if a person is travelling a lonely road somewhere, and fear seizes him'.

As noted, Greek medicine, with its routine binary

6 *Melencolia* by A. Dürer, 1514. A despondent winged female figure holding a geometrical instrument surrounded by attributes associated with knowledge. The sands of time are running out; nature too is in decay.

thinking, singled out two main manifestations of mood and behavioural disturbance, mania and melancholia. The fullest early clinical descriptions of these were advanced by a contemporary of the great Galen, Aretaeus of Cappadocia (AD *c.*150–200), in his *On the Causes and Signs of Diseases*. He observed of one case of melancholy:

> Sufferers are dull or stern: dejected or unreasonably torpid, without any manifest cause: such is the commencement of melancholy, and they also become peevish, dispirited, sleepless, and start up from a disturbed sleep. Unreasonable fears also seize them. . . . They are prone to change their mind readily, to become base, mean-spirited, illiberal, and in a little time perhaps simple, extravagant, munificent not from any virtue of the soul but from the changeableness of the disease. But if the illness become more urgent, hatred, avoidance of the haunts of men, vain lamentations are seen: they complain of life and desire to die; in many the understanding so leads to insensibility and fatuousness that they become ignorant of all things and forgetful of themselves and live the life of inferior animals.

Melancholia, as is evident from this clinical account, was not, as it would later be for Keats and other Romantic poets, a fashionably dreamy sadness. For Aretaeus and for Classical medicine in general, it was a severe mental disturbance. Anguish and dejection were its essential elements, but also involved were powerful emotions springing from hallucinations and sensations of suspicion, mistrust, anxiety, and trepidation. 'The patient may imagine he has taken another form than his own,' Aretaeus commented on the delusions of the depressed:

> one believes himself a sparrow; a cock or an earthen vase; another a God, orator or actor, carrying gravely a stalk of straw and imagining himself holding a sceptre of the World; some utter cries of an infant and demand to be carried in arms, or they believe themselves a grain of mustard, and tremble continuously for fear of being eaten by a hen.

Similar tropes—one man too terrified to urinate in case he drowned the whole world, another sure he was made of glass and about to shatter at any moment—were recycled right through to Robert Burton's *Anatomy of Melancholy* (1621) and beyond.

For Aretaeus, depression was a grave condition, its delusions, obsessions, and *idées fixes* highly destructive. 'The melancholic isolates himself, he is afraid of being persecuted and imprisoned, he torments himself with superstitious ideas, he hates life . . . he is terror-stricken, he mistakes his fantasies for the truth . . . he complains of imaginary diseases, he curses life and wishes for death.'

At the opposite pole lay mania. A condition marked by excess and uncontrollability, it found vent, for Aretaeus, in 'fury, excitement and cheerfulness'. In acute forms, the sick person 'sometimes slaughters the servants'; or he might become grandiose: 'without being cultivated he says he is a philosopher.' Mania often included euphoria: the sufferer 'has deliriums, he studies astronomy, philosophy ... he feels great and inspired'.

Displaying the rationalist temper of Classical medicine, Aretaeus deplored those collective outbursts of frenzied cultic Dionysian activity which, to his mind, had disgraced Greek civilization and were still all too present in the Roman Empire, diagnosing these religious outbursts medically. He pinpointed the kinds of superstitious mania which involved possession by a god (divine *furor*), especially amongst those following the cult of Cybele (Juno). In 'enthusiastic and ecstatic states', devotees would stage wild processions, and, as with the Corybantics, believers 'would castrate themselves and then offer their penis to the goddess'. Zealots fell into trances supposedly derived from divine inspiration, feeling deliriously euphoric and worshipping the gods of ecstasy and the dance. All this, in his view, betrayed 'insanity . . . in an ill, drunken and confused soul'.

Aretaeus has been credited with identifying what were much later to be called bipolar disorders. 'Some patients after being melancholic have fits of mania', he observed, 'so that mania is like a variety of melancholy.' A person previously euphoric suddenly 'has a tendency to melancholy; he becomes, at the end of the attack, languid, sad, taciturn, he complains that he is worried about his future, he feels ashamed.' After the down phase, they might swing back to hyperactivity: 'they show off in public with crowned heads as if they were returning victorious from the games; sometimes they laugh and dance all day and all night.'

Aretaeus' very recognizable picture of wild mood-swings would have seemed perfectly familiar to the nineteenth-century French psychiatrists, Jean-Pierre Falret and Jules Baillarger, whose work on circular or double insanity pointed towards the modern category of manic-depressive psychosis (see Chapter 6). Yet we must beware the temptations of hindsight.

Graeco-Roman medicine offered a welter of therapies for the mad, sometimes at odds with each other. The physician Soranus recommended talking to the deranged; Celsus by contrast believed in shock treatment, suggesting isolating patients in total darkness and administering cathartics in hopes of frightening them back into health.

A continuing tradition

Medieval Islamic and Christian medicine honoured and followed the medical traditions begun by Hippocrates and systematized by Galen, Aretaeus, and others, and the accounts of madness advanced by medieval learned doctors essentially repeated them. In the herbals and leechbooks produced by early medieval monks, simplified Classical learning was intermingled with folk beliefs and magical remedies. Melancholia and mania dominated the diagnoses. Among the medievals, Bartholomaeus Anglicus, who taught in thirteenth-century Paris, in the Aretaean manner included under 'melancholia' such states as anxiety, hypochondriasis, depression, and delusion.

Greek-derived thinking retained its validity and vitality in the Renaissance. Denis Fontanon, a mid-sixteenth-century professor at Montpellier, then a major medical university, stated, apropos mania, that it 'occurs sometimes solely from the warmer temper of the brain without a harmful humour, and this is like what happens in drunkenness. It occasionally arises from stinging and warm humours, such as yellow bile, attacking the brain and stimulating it along with its membranes.' Addressing its varieties, he explained their distinct features and causes. It was a good sign if mania involved laughter; whereas when the mixture of blood and choler (yellow bile) was 'burned'—that is, appeared especially heavy and thickened—there would be 'brutal madness and this is the most dangerous mania of all'.

Fontanon's younger contemporary at Montpellier, Felix Platter (1536–1614), similarly identified mania with excess. As in melancholia, its victims would 'imagine, judge and remember things falsely'. The maniac would also 'do everything unreasonably':

Sometimes they are the authors of relatively modest words and deeds which are not accompanied by raving; but more frequently, changed into rage, they express their mental impulse in a wild expression and in word and deed. Then they come out with false, obscene and horrible things, exclaim, swear, and with a certain brutal appetite, undertake different things, some of them very unheard of for men under any circumstances, even to the point of bestiality, behaving like animals. Some of them seek sexual satisfaction particularly intensely. I saw this happen to a certain noble matron, who was in every other way most honorable, but who invited by the

7 The sixteenth-century Swiss physician, Felix Platter, is shown seated, with two companions, at a table covered with surgical instruments and books. Below are the figures of Hippocrates and Galen, on either side of flayed human skin.

basest words and gestures men and dogs to have sex with her.

In his portrait of melancholia, Platter foregrounded anxiety and delusion. Echoing Aretaeus, he cast it as a 'kind of mental alienation, in which imagination and judgement are so perverted that without any cause the victims become very sad and fearful'. The disorder thus involved a crazy gothic castle of delusion founded upon false images.

Another contemporary, Timothie Bright, published the first English treatise on melancholia in 1586—Shakespeare's familiarity with psychiatric writings probably came through reading Bright. The climax of the humoral approach to mental disorder lies, however, in the encyclopaedic *Anatomy of Melancholy* (1621) by Robert Burton, an Oxford don who spent his entire life researching, writing, and revising his *magnum opus*. In creating a gloomy portrait-gallery of taciturn, solitary, deluded, and often dangerous melancholics, Burton, in addition to the classic distemperature of the spleen, brain, and blood, included the following possible causes or precipitants of the condition: 'idleness, solitariness, overmuch study, passions, perturbations, discontents, cares, miseries, vehement desires, ambitions, etc.'. His encyclopaedic curative recommendations similarly ran the gamut of remedies suggested ever since the Ancients: diet, exercise, distraction, travel, purgatives, bloodletting, and so on, including literally hundreds of herbal remedies. Marriage was the best cure for melancholy maids, wrote the bachelor Burton, and he also urged music therapy, which went back at least to Old Testament times:

> And it came to pass, when the evil spirit from God was upon Saul, that David took the harp, and played with his hand: so Saul was refreshed, and was well, and the evil spirit departed from him. (1 Sam. 16: 23)

Like many other writers on the subject, Burton was himself a sufferer: 'I write of melancholy by being busy to avoid melancholy.' And with an eye to fellow sufferers, his mammoth work concluded with the admonition, 'Be not solitary, be not idle', advice the author himself had evidently but half-followed. Burton's great work conveys the melancholy impression that there are as many theories of insanity as there are mad people, and that they all contradict each other: Polonius vindicated once more! The Renaissance thus brought no Copernican revolution in psychiatry, which would finally lay bare the secret motions beneath the skull. It was rather the culmination, and the conclusion, of the Classical tradition. In the century after Burton, the new

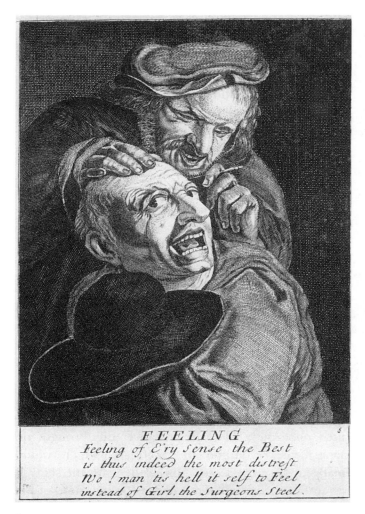

FEELING

Feeling of E'ry sense the Best
is thus indeed the most distress
Wo! man 'tis hell it self to Feel
instead of Girl, the Surgeons Steel.

8 *The Stone of Folly* by Teniers, seventeenth-century engraving. An itinerant surgeon extracting stones from a grimacing patient's head symbolizes the extraction of 'folly' (insanity).

anatomy and physiology associated with Andreas Vesalius and William Harvey was to usher in new organic theories of insanity to replace the humours, as will be shown in Chapter 6. Meanwhile developments in philosophy would open up new psychological approaches.

Towards a psychology

Late in the eighteenth century the British mad-doctor William Pargeter conjured up the maniac thus:

> Let us then figure to ourselves the situation of a fellow creature destitute of the guidance of that governing principle, reason—which chiefly distinguishes us from the inferior animals around us. . . . View man deprived of that noble endowment, and see in how melancholy a posture he appears.

Implicit in Pargeter's moving depiction is, of course, the ideal from which the madman had fallen, the paragon of *homo rationalis*. Plato had gloried in the rational soul; medieval theologians had alternately praised and reviled human reason (faith was what a believer needed). Marsilio Ficino, Pico della Mirandola, and other writers of the Italian Renaissance held that man's superiority to the animals on the Great Chain of Being lay in reason, further extolling the rational civilized male over women, children, and peasants. It was in the seventeenth century above all, however, that the mind became cardinal to philosophical models of man.

The seminal rationalist in that movement was René Descartes (1594–1650), who convinced himself that reason alone could rescue mankind from drowning in ignorance, confusion, and error. Descartes was born in Normandy and educated by the Jesuits, who introduced him to philosophy, mathematics, and physics. On 10 November 1619, in a quasi-mystical experience recorded in his *Discourse on Method* (1637), he dedicated his life to the pursuit of truth, resolving to be systematically sceptical about all received knowledge, so as to reconstruct philosophy on the basis of self-evident first principles. Building on the one thing which was beyond doubt—his own consciousness (*Cogito, ergo sum*: I am thinking, therefore I exist)—he aspired on that basis to establish principles so clear and distinct 'that the mind of man cannot doubt their truth'.

Like all later 'mechanical' philosophers, Descartes was determined that the Ptolemaic/Aristotelian cosmos of 'imaginary' qualities and 'fictional' elements should be replaced by a 'new philosophy', solidly grounded in reality: one composed of particles of matter in motion obeying mathematical laws. Logic required the division of Creation into two radically distinct categories, matter, that is 'extension' (including body), and mind. Spiritual beings like angels aside, humans alone possessed conscious minds; the behaviour of animals was completely explicable in terms of matter and motion—they were sophisticated machines or automata, devoid of will, feeling, or consciousness. The *appearance* of such attributes in brutes was due to reflexes—the reflex concept was prominent in his pioneering mechanistic account of the nervous system.

Descartes equated mind with the incorporeal soul: it was what conferred upon humans their consciousness, moral responsibility, and immortality. Although, being immaterial, it could not be identified with or located in space ('extension'), he held that the mind docked with the body at the pineal gland, a unitary structure seated in mid-brain. After Descartes' death, different areas of the brain—including the *medulla oblongata* (Malpighi, Willis), the *corpora striata* (Vieussens), and the *corpus callosum* (Lancisi)—were touted as the true seat of the soul by physicians unimpressed by the pineal gland.

Though Descartes thus radically rethought philosophy and medicine, he never explained to critics' satisfaction how mind and body could actually interact—his speculative localization in the pineal gland merely seemed to compound the problem, both physiologically and metaphysically. Mind had thus not been elucidated but had been rendered a mysterious ghost in the machine—though his account of the passions as mediating between mind and body was, in truth, more holistic than his mind/body dualism seemed to sanction. In many subsequent speculations about madness, mental disorder was put down to the complexities, or obscurities, of how mind and brain, or mind and body, touched base with each other. Jonathan Swift and other satirists diverted themselves with outlandish speculations as to how thoughts got distorted or derailed on their travels through the gland.

Overall, therefore, Cartesian dualism posed an audacious challenge—one with momentous medical consequences for reasoning about madness, since it implied that as consciousness was inherently and definitionally rational, insanity, precisely like regular physical illnesses, must derive from the body, or be a consequence of some very precarious connections in the brain. Safely somatized in this way, it could no longer be regarded as diabolical in origin or as threatening the integrity and salvation of the immortal soul, and became unambiguously a legitimate object of philosophical and medical enquiry.

While Descartes was not one himself, his thinking encouraged materialists, who went further and denied the reality of anything at all in the universe except matter. To orthodox Christians, the most threatening such materialist was Thomas Hobbes (1588–1679), who drew inspiration from Galileo and Descartes and played on the shocking implications of a mechanistic physiology and a materialist and reductionist psychology.

Hobbes deemed the universe a material continuum, utterly devoid of spirit, under a God who was characterized primarily by power. Knowledge was derived exclusively from sense impressions, and behaviour determined by physical laws of matter in motion, grounded in self-preservation: emotion was, in reality, motion. This materialist reading of human action as moved entirely by external sense-inputs permitted Hobbes to dismiss religious beliefs about spirits and witches as hallucinations spawned by the fevered operations of the brain. By extension, religion itself was a form of delusion. Insanity was thus erroneous thought caused by some defect in the body's machinery.

In his *Essay Concerning Human Understanding* (1690), John Locke too, like Hobbes, mounted a critique of Platonic or Cartesian innate ideas or pure reason, and taught that all ideas originate from sense impressions (via sight, taste, touch, hearing, smell). Originating like a blank sheet of paper (*tabula rasa*), the mind is informed and shaped by experience and nurtured by education.

False beliefs—amongst these Locke included 'witches' and 'goblins'—are the products of mis-associations of ideas. Madness is thus neither diabolical nor humoral but essentially delusional, a fault in cognition rather than in will or passion. 'Mad Men', explained Locke, 'put wrong Ideas together, and so make wrong Propositions, but argue and reason right from them; But Idiots make very few or no Propositions, but argue and reason scarce at all.' In due course, Lockean thinking, so highly esteemed in the Enlightenment, would form the basis of new secular and psychological approaches to understanding insanity. The implied equation he drew between delusion and faulty education instilled optimism: the mad could be retrained to think correctly.

Amongst seventeenth-century philosophers, madness was thus increasingly identified not with demons, humours, or even passions, but with irrationality, in models of mind which made the guarantee of soundness of mind the rational self. Despite this championing of reason, however, mental order and disorder remained Sphinxian mysteries. Paradoxically, the riddles of psyche/soma affinities had been reopened by the great clarifications Descartes had struggled to effect. Addressing hysteria, the notable eighteenth-century physician William Heberden thus expressed a reluctance to dogmatize about the root-causes of such mysterious, chameleon-like conditions, on account of 'our great ignorance of the connexion and sympathies of body and mind'. The attempts of later thinkers to resolve these intractable, even maddening, dilemmas will be explored in Chapter 6.

Fools and folly

To reason with a lunatic is folly
(George Man Burrows,
Commentaries on Insanity, 1828)

Stigma

All societies judge some people mad: any strict clinical
justification aside, it is part of the business of marking
out the different, deviant, and perhaps dangerous. Such
'stigma', according to the American sociologist Erving
Goffman, is 'the situation of the individual who is dis-
qualified from full social acceptance'. Stigmatizing—the
creation of spoiled identity—involves projecting onto an
individual or group judgements as to what is inferior,
repugnant, or disgraceful. It may thus translate disgust
into the disgusting and fears into the fearful, first by
singling out difference, next by calling it inferiority,
and finally by blaming 'victims' for their otherness.

This demonizing process may be regarded as psychologically and anthropologically driven, arising out of deep-seated and perhaps unconscious needs to order the world by demarcating self from other, as in the polarized distinctions we draw between Insiders and Outsiders, Black and White, Natives and Foreigners, Gay and Straight, Pure and Polluted, and so forth. The construction of such 'them-and-us' oppositions reinforces our fragile sense of self-identity and self-worth through the pathologization of pariahs.

Setting the sick apart sustains the fantasy that we are whole. Disease diagnosis thus constitutes a powerful classificatory tool, and medicine contributes its fair share to the stigmatizing enterprise. Amongst those scapegoated and anathematized by means of this cognitive apartheid, the 'insane' have, of course, been conspicuous. This polarizing of the sane and the crazy in turn spurred and legitimized the institutionalizing trend which, as will be discussed in Chapter 5, gathered momentum from the seventeenth century.

Witty fools?

Folk wisdom has assumed that madness is as madness looks, a view which, in its turn, has been bolstered by artists and writers. In jokes and on the stage, the insane have standardly been depicted as strange and dishevelled—as 'wild men', with straw in their hair and their clothes threadbare, ripped or fantastical, or sometimes wearing barely a stitch. Further conventions have rammed such messages home. Just as the cuckold was known by his horns, so it was standard for the fool to be portrayed as disfigured by a stone protruding from his forehead, the 'stone of folly': the character flaw was thus written all over the face. Jesters and stage buffoons bespoke folly too, through their cap and bells, bladder and pinwheel, motley and hobbyhorse. Got up in a similar 'uniform' of their own, ex-patients of Bethlem Hospital tramped the highways, licensed to beg—their numbers being swollen by opportunistic sane mendicants who, like Edgar in *King Lear*, masqueraded as Bedlamites. They might sing for their supper, and their songs were even printed as 'Bedlam ballads':

> I'll bark against the Dog-Star
> I'll crow away the morning,
> I'll chase the moon till it be noon
> And I'll make her leave her horning . . .

In the culture of madness 'reality' and 'representations' endlessly played off each other. What a crazy world in

JOHN DONALDSON,

A Poor Idiot who usually walked before Funeral Procefsions at Edinburgh.

Published by Henry Sawyer, Dean S.t Soho.

9 John Donaldson, a poor idiot who lived in the eighteenth century and who made it his habit to walk before funeral processions at Edinburgh.

which the poor had to pretend to be mad in order to get a crust!

Certain stereotypes have exercised a powerful and lasting fascination. Alongside those models already mentioned in Chapter 2—for instance, the hubristic hero punished by the gods by loss of his reason—Greek thinkers advanced the idea of divine madness in the artist, 'inspired' (literally 'filled with spirit') or touched by a divine 'fire'. Notably in the *Phaedrus*, Plato spoke of the 'divine fury' of the poet, and works attributed to Aristotle (384–322 BC) sketched the profile of the melancholy genius, whose solitary discontent fired his imagination to produce works of originality.

Such views were revived in the Renaissance by Ficino and other humanists; to dub a poet 'mad' was, in the conventions of the age, to pay him a compliment. Michael Drayton thus praised the dramatist Kit Marlowe:

> For that fine madness still he did retain,
> Which rightly should possess a poet's brain.

Shakespeare for his part suggested in *A Midsummer Night's Dream* that 'the lunatick, the lover and the poet are of imagination all compact', and thus described the act of creation:

The poet's eye in a fine phrensy rolling
Doth glance from heav'n to earth, from earth to heav'n
And, as imagination bodies forth
The forms of things unknown, the poet's pen
Turns them to shape, and gives to aiery nothing
A local habitation and a name.

And similar views were later rhymed after the Restoration by John Dryden:

Great wits are sure to madness near allied,
And thin partitions do their bounds divide.

Visiting what was facetiously dubbed the 'Academy of Bedlam', the diarist John Evelyn found one inmate 'mad with making verses'. It was a standard crack: writers were supposedly mad, and those who were mad suffered from the *cacoethes scribendi*, the writer's itch.

Renaissance artists were credited with receiving visions in dreams and daydreams; gloom and woe fired the poet's fancy; and, especially on the stage, there skulked the melancholy malcontent, clad all in black, disaffected, disdainful, dangerous, yet brilliantly discerning and diamond sharp. For Hamlet in the churchyard or Jaques in the forest of Arden in *As You Like It*, something bittersweet was to be savoured in a contemplative sorrow: Jaques enjoyed sucking 'melancholy out of a stone'. The same idea underlay Thomas Gray's *Elegy*

Written in a Country Churchyard in the eighteenth century. Given man's mortality, the wheel of fortune, and
the scurviness of the times, what other response could
there be to life's changes and chances but a detached
sadness?—such was the drift of Robert Burton's
obsessive *Anatomy of Melancholy* (1621):

> When I go musing all alone,
> Thinking of divers things fore-known,
> When I build Castles in the air,
> Void of sorrow and void of fear,
> Pleasing my self with phantasms sweet,
> Methinks the time runs very fleet.
> All my joys to this are folly,
> Naught so sweet as Melancholy.

For Burton, to live in this sordid, base world, surrounded by despots, tyrants, misers, thieves, slanderers,
adulterers, and whole broods of knaves and fools was a
melancholy matter. Hence his pen name 'Democritus
Junior', after the Greek philosopher who became a solitary because he found mankind alternately so risible
and so pitiable. Life was a black comedy.

Amongst the paradoxes beloved of the Humanists
was the thought that, in a mad world, the only realist
was the 'fool' or simpleton. In *The Praise of Folly* (1511),
Erasmus's eponymous heroine, so full of herself, prated

wisdom unthinkingly, while the Fool in *King Lear* and Feste in *Twelfth Night* outwitted logic in nonsense ditties which gave voice to darker truths denied to sober speech. In sixteenth-century France Michel de Montaigne, who posed the sceptical question, 'what do I know?', thought the whole world run mad, or at least hinted that all humans, since the Fall, lived at risk of Reason's shipwreck or the poison of the passions.

Aboard this ship of fools or topsy-turvy world, scholars were crazy and (in Gray's phrase) it was folly to be wise for, as the Acts of the Apostles warned, 'much learning doth make thee mad'. Cervantes explains in *Don Quixote* how his hidalgo hero embarked upon his career of tilting at windmills:

> this gentleman, in the times when he had nothing to do—as was the case for most of the year—gave himself up to the reading of books of knight errantry; which he loved and enjoyed so much that he almost entirely forgot his hunting, and even the care of his estate.

Evidently he should have heeded Burton's advice: be not solitary, be not idle.

Madness thus donned many disguises and acted out a bewildering multiplicity of parts in early modern times: moral and medical, negative and positive, religious and secular. After all, man was an 'amphibian', part angel, part beast, and hence a divided self—and in any case was fallen: no wonder his pretensions were mocked by madness.

The conundrums and contradictions in this riddling doubling of *homo sapiens* with the mad fool—'s*emel insanivimus omnes*', Burton declared: we're all mad—are embodied in the double face of Bethlem Hospital, both a bricks-and-mortar institution on the edge of London and an image ('Bedlam'). Since that 'College' was open to visitors, the sane and the mad were there brought tantalizingly face-to-face: who could tell the difference? For its many critics, the fact that Bethlem allowed itself to be included among the 'shows of London', like the menagerie in the Tower, was central to its scandal: putting the Other on display in a human zoo or freak show courted shameless voyeurism, as is suggested in a host of Bedlam cartoons, especially the final scene of Hogarth's *The Rake's Progress*, where two visiting ladies of fashion (or are they high-class courtesans?) linger before the cell of the mad monarch: who is really crazy?

Officially at least, Bethlem's insane were meant to be edifying spectacles, object lessons to the public at large of the wages of passion, vice, and sin. In 1753, a magazine held that there was no 'better lesson [to] be taught us in any part of the globe than in this school of misery. Here we may see the mighty reasoners of the earth,

The HOSPITAL _of_ BETHLEHEM.   L'HOSPITAL _de_ Fov.

Printed for John Bowles & Son, at the Black Horse in Cornhil.

10 The Hospital of Bethlem (Bedlam) at Moorfields. This is the second building of the Bethlem Hospital (Bedlam), built in 1675–6 at Moorfields, just north of the City of London. It was designed by the natural philosopher, Robert Hooke. Its showy and palatial exterior was the subject of much satirical comment.

below even the insects that crawl upon it; and from so humbling a sight we may learn to moderate our pride.' Without self-control, who might not plunge into the depths of derangement? Indeed, as critics loved to note, it could be hard to tell visitors and patients apart, and the mad inmates might even be held up as more free and fortunate (and hence sensible) than those outside. Recounting a supposed visit, the journalist Ned Ward pictured one of the Bedlamites

> holding forth with much vehemence against Kingly government. I told him he deserv'd to be hang'd for talking of treason. 'Now', says he, 'you're a fool, for we madmen have as much privilege of speaking our minds . . . you may talk what you will, and nobody will call you in question for it. Truth is persecuted everywhere abroad, and flies thither for sanctuary, where she sits as safe as a knave in a church, or a whore in a nunnery. I can use here as I please and that's more than you dare to'.

The archetypal Bedlam situation was milked in *The Rake's Progress* sequence. In the early scenes, Hogarth's hero Tom Rakewell drinks, gambles, whores, and marries his way through two fortunes. Finally, demented and dumped in Bethlem, he lies naked, a brutalized wreck, surrounded by his fellow crazies: a mad lover

11 At the centre of the print from Hogarth's *Rake's Progress* series is Tom Rakewell, who, having gambled away his fortune, has knocked over his chair and fallen to his knees, wigless and frantic, with the dog barking at him. Madness will follow, symbolized by the fire breaking out in the wainscoting; after 1735.

('love sickness' had long featured in the roster of insanity), a mad bishop, a mad king (a *pretender*?), sitting with
make-believe orb and sceptre on his close-stool of a
throne, a popish religious enthusiast, a mad tailor, and
a crazy astronomer, gazing up to the rafters through a
rolled-up paper 'telescope'.

Is this what the Bedlamites looked like? *That* is clearly
not Hogarth's point: the parable he was telling was
about the *British*. Indeed, on the far wall, a mad artist
(Hogarth himself?) sketches a coin of the realm, with
'Britannia 1763' inscribed around its rim. Hogarth thus
pretends to engrave Bethlem while actually depicting
Britain. He is not mocking the mad to spare the sane,
he is holding up the mirror to the viewer: it is we who
are mad—or, in the words of the moralizing Baptist
Thomas Tryon, 'the World is but a great *Bedlam*, where
those that are *more mad*, lock up those that are *less*'.

Jokes about mad monarchs came home to roost
remarkably rapidly: George III's delirious descent in
1788 provided a golden opportunity for satirists and
cartoonists like James Gillray to highlight the craziness
of power. The politician Edmund Burke was so obsessive as to be thought well nigh certifiable—'the most
eloquent madman I know', joked Edward Gibbon. His
fellow Whig politician Charles James Fox likewise: his
unkempt looks, impetuous political switches, and

12 Plate VIII from Hogarth's *Rake's Progress* series, 1735. Now insane, Tom Rakewell sits on the floor of the gallery at Bethlem Hospital, London, grasping at his head in the classic pose of the maniac. His faithful admirer, Sarah Young, cries at the spectacle whilst two attendants attach chains to his legs; they are surrounded by other lunatics.

passionate enthusiasm for the French Revolution led cartoonists to represent him as quite out of his wits. One engraving pictures him blanketed in Bedlam. Wearing a crown of straw and clutching an impromptu sceptre, he exhibits weird delusions of grandeur: 'Do you not behold friend Sam I have obtained the height of all my wishes?' he buttonholes a visitor.

Disinheriting folly

In time, the medicalization of insanity, the move to lock mad people up, and the sensibilities of the age of reason undermined and rendered obsolete the old figure of the 'witty fool' with his riddling truths and carnivalesque freedoms. The writing is clearly on the wall in the following vignette written by the Newtonian physician Nicholas Robinson in the 1720s:

> It is not long ago since a very learned and ingenious Gentleman, so far started from his Reason, as to believe, that his Body was metamorphos'd into a Hobby-Horse, and nothing would serve his Turn, but that his Friend, who came to see him, must mount his Back and ride. I must confess, that all the philosophy I was Master of, could not dispossess him of this Conceit; 'till by application of generous Medicines, I

restor'd the disconcerted nerves to their regular
Motions, and, by that Means, gave him a Sight of his
Error.

Hobby–horses are obviously out, and the implied sexual
licence inadmissible. For the likes of Robinson, folly is
no longer revealing, meaningful, or amusing, it simply
needs a strong purge.

The playful ambiguities of Erasmian irony and
double-talk—Folly as teacher—were no longer tenable
as science turned insanity into pathology and the rise of
the asylum set the mad poet or artist at growing risk
of being put under lock and key, for society's good, or
even his own. James Carkesse was a clerk at the Navy
Office under the diarist Samuel Pepys. A casualty of
office politics, he grew disturbed and was locked up first
in a private madhouse and later in Bethlem under its
physician Dr Allen. There he wrote a collection of verse,
published in 1679 under the title *Lucida Intervalla*. This
drew upon the old conceits of mad poetry—following
the Erasmian tradition of 'praisers of folly', the privilege of the badge of lunacy is used to lash a crazy world;
and yet paradoxically and self-defeatingly, Carkesse's
verse also sought to deny the author's own identity as a
mad poet. This ambivalence appears in contradictory
titles: one poem is headed 'Poets are Mad', another,

'Poets no Lunatick'—and in the 'lucid intervals' blazoned in the title.

Physicians are the ones who are crazy, proclaimed Carkesse, but Bedlamites are sane, or at least would be but for the treatment they suffer:

> Says He, who more wit than the Doctor had,
> Oppression will make a wise man Mad;

—the reference is to Solomon in the Old Testament. Carkesse protested his sanity: what was mistaken for lunacy in him, was actually poetic inspiration:

> The truth on't is, my Brain's well fixt condition
> Apollo better knows, than his Physitian:
> 'Tis Quacks disease, not mine, my poetry
> By the blind Moon-Calf, took for Lunacy.

But Dr Allen (here dubbed 'Mad-quack') had informed him 'that till he left making Verses, he was not fit to be discharg'd'. What did this prove but Dr Mad-quack's folly? For poetry was neither the source nor a symptom of madness, but therapeutic; after all, wasn't Apollo the god of both poetry and healing?

In Augustan culture, madness remained a favourite metaphor. By Swift, Pope, and other Tory poets and critics, the outpourings of Grub-Street hacks and 'dunces' were damned as deranged—they had no touch of the divine about them, precisely because, far from being a gift from on high, their 'inspiration' welled up from their bowels. Their much-prized 'afflatus' was mere flatulence, issuing from diseased guts, or it came from what Pope called 'a morbid secretion from the brain'. 'The corruption of the senses is the creation of the spirit', pronounced Swift in a dark aphorism. It was, in other words, only *false* and *contemptible* versifiers who were deranged: true poetry by contrast flowed from healthy minds: the Dean prided himself on being 'a perfect stranger to the spleen'.

Great writers were cast as sane by an Augustan aesthetics which construed the artist not as a visionary but as a supreme craftsman. The mad poet lost his licence to conjure with words, and the Aristotelian trope of poetic melancholy was parodied in Pope's *Dunciad* nightmare of Grub Street hacks skulking in their Cave of Spleen infected with the *cacoethes scribendi* and obsessed by 'the power of noise'. Swift's anti-heroes—the first-person unreliable narrators of *Gulliver's Travels* and *A Tale of a Tub*—were garrulous windbags, full of themselves, compulsively and solipsistically digressing and lacking true self-awareness. The *Tale*'s hero expresses the demented hope that he will eventually be able 'to write upon nothing'. In his satires, Swift saw lunacy infecting Dissenters and free-thinkers, scientists and projectors, and his notorious *Modest Proposal* (1729), suggesting as it did that Ireland's economic and demographic problems could be solved at a stroke by serving up babies for dinner, could have been written by a Lockean madman reasoning correctly from false premises.

Madness and genius

As if taking the hint, the poets of the age of reason generally did not seek to don the mantle of madness. The age held genius in esteem, to be sure, but found it in balance and good sense. While prizing originality, William Sharpe's *A Dissertation upon Genius* (1755) and Edward Young's *Conjectures on Original Composition* (1759) read creativity as the outpourings of the healthy psyche, analogous to the growth and flowering of plants.

In their turn, Romantic poets worshipped the imagination as the noblest work of man. Denouncing the empiricist model of the mind identified with Locke as grossly mechanistic, William Blake pronounced that 'art is the tree of life'. That visionary engraver and poet gloried in the idea of the mad artist, recording a dream in which the poet William Cowper 'came to me and said: "O that I were insane always. I will never rest. Can you not make me truly insane? . . . You retain health and yet are as mad as any of us all—over us all—mad as a refuge from unbelief—from Bacon, Newton and Locke." ' But Blake was exceptional. Staking their claim for the poet as the legislator of humanity, the Romantics as a whole saw the writer not as psychologically peculiar but as truly healthy—indeed, Charles Lamb wrote an essay entitled 'The Sanity of True Genius'.

This Romantic ideal of the heroic, healthy genius was later daringly or recklessly abandoned in *fin de siècle* degenerationism. Associating mental disturbance with various other illnesses (syphilis, tuberculosis) and vices (drinking, drug-taking), the avant-garde, notably in the Paris of Flaubert, Baudelaire, Verlaine, and Rimbaud, held that true art—as opposed to the good taste favoured by the bourgeoisie—sprang from the morbid and pathological: sickness and suffering fired and liberated the spirit, perhaps with the aid of hashish, opium, and absinthe, and works of genius were hammered out on the anvil of pain.

From the psychiatric viewpoint, the Italian Cesare Lombroso held that, as a breed, artists and writers were disturbed and perhaps in need of treatment. Along similar lines, J. F. Nisbet's *The Insanity of Genius* (1900) offered a backhanded celebration of 'men of letters lapsing into or approaching insanity—Swift, Johnson, Cowper, Southey, Shelley, Byron, Campbell, Goldsmith, Charles Lamb, Walter Savage Landor, Rousseau, Chatterton, Pascal, Chateaubriand, George Sand, Tasso, Alfieri, Edgar Allen Poe'.

In his own way Freud perpetuated this *fin de siècle* stigmatization by deeming art the child of neurosis, which made Virginia Woolf fearful of his designs: psychoanalysis, if it worked, would toll the knell of the novelist. And the American poet Ezra Pound later accused the public:

> It has been your habit for long to do away with good writers,
> You either drive them mad, or else blink at their suicides,
> Or else you condone their drugs, and talk of insanity and genius,
> But I will not go mad to please you.

The breakdowns (sometimes followed by suicide) of such creative figures as Antonin Artaud, Nijinsky, Woolf, Sylvia Plath, and Anne Sexton further fuelled the mad/genius debate. 'As an experience', declared Woolf, 'madness is terrific I can assure you, and not to be sniffed at; and in its lava I still find most of the things I write about. It shoots out of one everything shaped, final not in mere driblets, as sanity does.' In our own time Kay Redfield Jamison's *Touched with Fire:*

Manic-Depressive Illness and the Artistic Temperament (1998)—the reflections of a manic-depressive academic psychiatrist—and the writings of the neurologist Oliver Sacks show there is still much life in the 'creative malady' controversy.

Nerves

Meantime the cultural stereotype of the melancholic also underwent many modifications. Through such works as Richard Blackmore's *Treatise of the Spleen and Vapours* (1725) and George Cheyne's *The English Malady* (1733), the nervous, narcissistic valetudinarian became a fashionable if absurd Enlightenment figure. The Scot Cheyne identified his 'English malady', a form of depression, as the disorder of the elite in an advanced, prosperous, competitive nation: the pursuit of affluence, novelty, and elegance, and the enjoyment of the 'good life'— excessive eating and drinking—exacted a heavy toll.

Doubtless with his own 'case' in mind—gormandizing at one point blew him up to 450 lbs— Cheyne noted that '*Great Wits* are generally great *Epicures*, at least, Men of *Taste*'. If the stimuli of the bottle and the table were needed in order to shine, no wonder the nerves became damaged.

13 A depressed scholar surrounded by mythological figures, representing the melancholy temperament. The main image shows a scholar with a knife behind him and a goddess with an apple (fruit of knowledge) before him. In the bottom left-hand corner is Minerva, goddess of wisdom, and at the top is an owl, one of her attributes. The price of wisdom is melancholy.

Sickness, held Cheyne, made terrible inroads into the sensibilities of those fine spirits blessed, or cursed, with exquisite feelings and hyperactive brains. The highly strung were spinning dizzyingly downwards. Fleeing '*Anxiety* and *Concern*', they sought diversion in dissipation—'*Assemblies*, Musick Meetings, Plays, Cards, and *Dice*', which jeopardized their health. The irony (or cosmic justice), in short, was that it was the Quality, the social and literary elite, who were chiefly doomed to suffer: just as melancholy had once been 'the courtier's coat of arms', now clodhopping peasants alone were spared the English malady.

In his *Treatise of the Hypochondriack and Hysterick Diseases* (1730), the Dutch-born practitioner and satirist Bernard Mandeville examined the kind of modish melancholy with which the elite liked to flirt, by means of a fictitious dialogue between a physician and a gentleman patient who explained how reading about illness had reduced him to hypochondria.

As the fashionable Bath doctor James Makittrick Adair declared in 1790,

Upwards of thirty years ago, a treatise on nervous diseases was published by my quondam learned and ingenious preceptor Dr. WHYTT, professor of physic, at Edinburgh. Before the publication of this book, people of fashion had not the least idea that they had nerves;

but a fashionable apothecary of my acquaintance, having cast his eye over the book, and having been often puzzled by the enquiries of his patients concerning the nature and causes of their complaints, derived from thence a hint, by which he readily cut the gordian knot—'*Madam, you are nervous!*' The solution was quite satisfactory, the term became fashionable, and spleen, vapours, and hyp were forgotten.

From the eighteenth century onwards, polite society has continued to find in such 'nervous' disorders (the vapours, the spleen, and hysteria, now no longer viewed as uterine but as nervous in origin) a rich social idiom. While permitting display of superfine sensibilities, these complaints served as signs of social superiority, for the ailments were exclusive to truly refined temperaments. Such sufferers as himself, wrote James Boswell in the newspaper column he published under the pen name 'The Hypochondriack', might console themselves with the knowledge that their very miseries also marked their superiority. Far more vulnerable to 'the black dog' (depression) and anxious about what he deemed 'the dangerous prevalence of imagination', his friend and mentor Samuel Johnson thought him a silly ass for trifling with such nonsense. Soon George III was to be insisting that he was not 'mad but only nervous'.

Fashionable melancholy had a bright future ahead of

it in various incarnations. On both sides of the Atlantic, eminent Victorians sank or wallowed in hypochondria (mainly male) and hysteria (essentially for the ladies). By the *fin de siècle*, it was trendy to be 'neurasthenic', much as, in superior Manhattan circles, one might till very recently lose face unless engaged in 'analysis interminable' with a *chic* shrink. Private 'nerve' clinics, hydros, and spas sprang up for rich breakdown cases in Europe and America alike, paralleling the TB sanatoria in the Alps.

The glamorization of the gloomy genius had traditionally been a male preserve, as versified in John Milton's *Il Penseroso* (1632) and Matthew Green's *The Spleen* (1737). More recently, and perhaps as an ironic upshot of, or backlash against, the movement for female emancipation gathering momentum from the mid-nineteenth century, women have come to dominate the cultural stereotyping of mental disorder—and they have been disproportionately the recipients of mental treatments, both within and beyond custodial institutions. The autobiographical novels of Mary Wollstonecraft (1759–97) developed the gothic image of the mad and/or victimized heroine; sentimental fiction popularized the Ophelia figure, the young lady disappointed in love doomed to a hysterical breakdown followed by an early and exquisite death; while the female maniac assumed prominence in Bertha Mason, the first Mrs Rochester (a 'clothed hyena') in Charlotte Brontë's *Jane Eyre* (1847). Depressive, hysterical, suicidal, and self-destructive behaviour thus became closely associated, from Victorian times, with stereotypes of womanhood in the writings of the psychiatric profession, in the public mind, and amongst women themselves. Freud himself classically asked: 'what do women want?', and went on to diagnose penis envy. Classic hysteria, so common in Freud's day, may also have disappeared, but it has perhaps metamorphosed into new and primarily female conditions, notably anorexia nervosa, somatization disorder, and bulimia.

The figure of Folly may have also taken her bow, but the original riddle remains: is the world mad, is civilization itself psychopathogenic?—the question, of course, posed by Freud's *Civilization and its Discontents* (1926). And if civilized society is thus disordered, what right has it to pass judgement on the 'insane'? Regarding his committal to Bethlem, the Restoration playwright Nathaniel Lee reputedly declared: 'They called me mad, and I called them mad, and damn them, they outvoted me.' The issue is still alive.

Locking up the mad

Before the asylum

The theory and practice of confining the insane in foundations designed exclusively for them came late. That is not, of course, to say that lunatics were till then exempt from regulation and control. Greek and Roman law sought to prevent them from destroying life, limb, and property, and made guardians responsible for them. 'If a man is mad', wrote Plato in the *Laws*, 'he shall not be at large in the city, but his family shall keep him in any way they can.'

Insanity was basically, in those days and for long after, a domestic responsibility—it remained so in Japan till well into the twentieth century. The seriously disturbed were kept at home, whilst the harmless might be allowed to wander, though as evil spirits were thought to fly out of them to possess others, the deranged were feared and shunned.

In Christian Europe too, it was the family which was held responsible for the deeds of its mad members, just as with children; lunatics and 'village idiots' typically remained in domestic care—often enough, neglect or cruelty—hidden away in a cellar or caged in a pigpen, sometimes under a servant's control. Or they were sent away, to wander the pathways and beg their crusts. Insanity was deeply shameful to a family, on account of its overtones of diabolical possession or of bad stock.

More formal segregation began to emerge towards the end of the Middle Ages, often inspired by the Christian duty of charity. Lunatics were sometimes locked in towers or dungeons under public auspices. In London the religious house of St Mary of Bethlehem, founded in 1247 and lastingly known as Bethlem ('Bedlam'), was catering for lunatics by the late fourteenth century. By then, the Flemish village of Gheel, which housed the shrine of St Dymphna, had gained a reputation as a healing centre for the disturbed. Asylums were also founded at an early date under religious auspices in fifteenth-century Spain, in Valencia, Zaragoza, Seville, Valladolid, Toledo, and Barcelona (the Islamic hospitals in Spain may have been the model).

Religious impulses stimulated many later foundations too, including the asylums set up in eighteenth-century Liverpool, Manchester, Newcastle, and York. In

14 This nineteenth-century print shows pilgrims receiving the Eucharist in the chapel of St Dymphna at Gheel. From medieval times, Gheel achieved fame as a healing shrine for the insane and mentally defective.

Catholic nations, institutions were staffed by brothers and sisters of charity, and the custody and care of the insane remained in the hands of religious orders in many countries right through into the twentieth century. In some nations, denominational differences led to polarized religious asylums, as with rival schooling systems: as late as the last quarter of the nineteenth century, separate Calvinist and Catholic asylums were being set up even in the 'modern' Netherlands.

A great confinement?

The state and its protocols also played a part. Michel Foucault famously argued in the 1960s that the rise of absolutism, typified by Louis XIV's France, inaugurated a Europe-wide 'great confinement' of the mad and poor, a movement of 'blind repression'. Scandalous to law and order, all those ne'er-do-wells tainted by 'unreason' became targets for sequestration in a vast street-sweeping operation. Paupers, petty criminals, layabouts, streetwalkers, vagabonds, and above all beggars formed the bulk of this monstrous army of the unreasonable, but symbolically their leaders were the insane and the idiotic. Already by the 1660s some 6,000 such undesirables were confined in Paris's Hôpital

Général alone. Such hospitals were soon cloned in the French provinces, and Foucault drew attention to comparable institutions elsewhere which shut troublesome people away not as a *therapeutic* but essentially as a *police* measure, a custodial act of state, notably the *Zuchthäuser* in German cities and England's workhouses and bridewells.

This 'great confinement', argued Foucault, amounted to more than physical sequestration, it also represented the debasement of madness itself. Hitherto, the mad had exercised a particular force and fascination, be it as a holy fool, witch, or as a man possessed. Half-wits and zanies had enjoyed the licence of free speech and the privilege of mocking their betters. Institutionalization, however, maintained Foucault, robbed madness of all such empowering features and reduced it to mere negation, an absence of humanity. Small wonder, he concluded, that madhouse inmates were likened to, and treated as, wild beasts in a cage: denied reason, that quintessential human attribute, what were they but brutes?

Though there is a certain plausibility in Foucault's interpretation, it is simplistic and over-generalized. With the exception of France, the seventeenth century did not bring any spectacular surge in institutionalization—it certainly did not become the automatic solution. Different nations and jurisdictions acted dissimilarly. Absolutist France did indeed centralize its responses to 'unreason'. From the Sun King's reign, it became the charge of civic authorities to provide facilities for the mad poor (later, under the Napoleonic Code, *préfects* assumed these responsibilities). Families could have mad kin legally restrained upon obtaining a *lettre de cachet* from royal officials, such warrants effectively depriving the lunatic of all legal rights.

In Russia, by contrast, state-organized receptacles for the insane hardly appeared at all before 1850, those who were confined being generally kept in monasteries. And across great swathes of rural Europe, few were psychiatrically institutionalized. Two lunatic asylums still sufficed for the whole of Portugal at the close of the nineteenth century, holding no more than about 600 inmates.

Nor does advanced England square with Foucault's 'great confinement', for state-led sequestration came late. Not until 1808 was an Act of Parliament passed even *permitting* the use of public funds for asylums, and not until 1845, and against those who denounced it as a waste of money or an infringement of freedom, was provision of such county asylums made mandatory. (At that date, there were still no asylums at all in Wales.) No more than around 5,000 people were held in 1800 in specialized lunatic asylums in a nation whose population was approaching ten millions—though there were perhaps as many lunatics again in workhouses, bridewells, and jails. There is little evidence that Parliament or the propertied classes saw 'unreason' as a dire threat.

In urbanized Europe, and in North America, the rise of the asylum is better seen not as an act of state but as a side effect of commercial and professional society. Growing surplus wealth encouraged the affluent to buy services—cultural, educational, medical—which once had been provided at home. Private madhouse keepers argued persuasively that seclusion was therapeutic. In England around 1800, the confined mad were largely housed in private asylums, operating for profit within the market economy in what was frankly termed the 'trade in lunacy'. In 1850, more than half were still in private institutions.

The early history of such private asylums is obscure, for they prized secrecy: families would wish to avoid publicity and only from 1774 were they required even to be legally licensed in England. Such receptacles go back, however, to the seventeenth century. When George Trosse went mad in the 1650s (see Chapter 2), his friends carried him off to a physician in Glastonbury who boarded the mad. After the Restoration,

15 In a lunatic asylum, surrounded by a variety of other deranged individuals, a half-naked patient, his wrists chained, is restrained by orderlies. The print (1735) is an obvious echo of Hogarth's *Rake's Progress* series, indicating the popularity of scenes out

newspapers began to carry advertisements for such 'private houses'. By 1800, licensed private madhouses totalled around fifty.

Early asylums came in all shapes and sizes, some well and others atrociously run. In no country before 1800 was medical supervision a legal requirement, nor did medical overlordship automatically ensure good care. The medical 'dynasty' of the Monros at Bethlem—Dr James Monro was succeeded by his son John, who was succeeded by his son Thomas, who was then succeeded by his son Edward, mirroring the four Georges who ran the nation—did not prevent that institution from becoming hidebound and corrupt: quite the opposite in fact. Some of the best initiatives were lay-led, notably the York Retreat (discussed below), whose high repute proved a thorn in the side of the medical profession's call for a medical monopoly. Nevertheless, a series of Acts passed from the 1820s required medical presence first in public and later in private asylums.

Some early madhouses were huge—several designed largely for paupers and army and navy casualties sprang up in the suburbs to the north-east of London, housing a couple of hundred patients each. Others were tiny: Dr Nathaniel Cotton's at St Albans, the 'Collegium Insanorum', housed no more than half a dozen in comfortable conditions. Charging up to five guineas a week—a year's wages for a servant—Cotton obviously catered for a better class of lunatic. Established in 1792, Ticehurst House in Sussex also provided de luxe psychiatry for the rich. Patients brought their own personal servants; a select few were lodged in individual houses in the grounds; and gentlemen lunatics were allowed to follow the hounds.

Foucault claimed that the great confinement essentially involved the sequestration of the mad poor by supporters of the bourgeois work ethic, and in his *Madmen and the Bourgeoisie: A Social History of Insanity and Psychiatry* (1981) Klaus Doerner followed suit. But there is little trace of organized labour in early asylums—indeed, critics accused them of being dens of idleness. And enterprising madhouse proprietors naturally sought rich and genteel patients, who would not be expected to work.

It would thus be simplistic to cast the rise of institutional psychiatry in crudely functional or conspiratorial terms, as a new witch-hunt or a tool of social control designed to smooth the running of emergent industrial society. The asylum solution should be viewed less in terms of central policy than as the site of myriad negotiations of wants, rights, and responsibilities, between diverse parties in a mixed consumer economy with a burgeoning service sector. The confinement (and subsequent release) of a sufferer was commonly less a matter of official fiat than the product of complex bargaining between families, communities, local officials, magistrates, and the superintendents themselves. The initiative to confine might come from varied sources; asylums were used by families no less than by the state; and the law could serve many interests. Something similar to the complex negotiation of interests which underlay and drove institutionalization in Georgian and early Victorian England is now being revealed in studies of asylums in twentieth-century Africa and Latin America.

Asylums varied widely in quality. Reformers exposed many as abominations, riddled with corruption and cruelty, where whips and chains masqueraded as therapeutic; and, as Chapter 7 shows, a patient protest literature expressed these charges. Yet asylums could also be supportive. Deranged after several suicide attempts, the poet William Cowper spent eighteen months in Nathaniel Cotton's St Albans asylum, just mentioned. His autobiography has nothing but praise for the care he received from a doctor 'ever watchful and apprehensive for my welfare', and he took one of the staff away with him to be his personal servant. The hundreds of pages of testimony given to the House of Commons Committee on Madhouses (1815) attest the merits of certain private houses, while baring the callous, grasping squalor of others.

Seedbed for psychiatry

The private madhouse served the 'trade in lunacy', but it also became a forcing-house for the development of psychiatry as an art and science. The asylum was not instituted for the practice of psychiatry; psychiatry rather was the practice developed to manage its inmates. Ideas about insanity remained abstract and theoretical before doctors and other proprietors gained extensive experience of handling the mad at close quarters in such houses. It had long been assumed that the mad were like wild beasts, requiring brutal taming, and stock therapies and drugs had been used time out of mind: physical restraint, bloodletting, purges, and vomits. Buoyed up by enlightened optimism, however, practical psychiatry was transformed through asylum experience, and the claim became standard that the well-designed, well-managed asylum was the machine to restore the insane to health. Experience and innovation became the watchwords.

An early champion of the asylum as a therapeutic engine was William Battie. Physician to London's new

16 A mentally ill patient in a straitjacket attached to the wall and a strange barrel-shaped contraption around his legs. Many different modes of restraint had been tried; most were found counterproductive, triggering the 'non-restraint' movement; photograph after a wood-engraving, 1908.

St Luke's Asylum and owner of a private asylum, Battie conceded in the 1750s that a fraction of the insane did indeed suffer from 'original insanity', which, like original sin, was incurable. Yet far more common was 'consequential insanity'—i.e. insanity resulting from events—for which the prognosis was favourable. To maximize cures, argued Battie and his many followers, what was required was early diagnosis and confinement (before the condition grew confirmed), and then a regime tailored to the individual case. Blanket therapeutics, like the annual spring bloodletting meted out at Bethlem, were useless; surgical and mechanical techniques would avail little; and 'medicine' would accomplish far less than 'management', by which was meant close person-to-person contact designed to treat the specific delusions or delinquencies of the individual. Contradicting the therapeutic gloom which typified Bethlem, Battie instilled a new enlightened optimism: 'madness is ... as manageable as many other distempers.'

The decades around 1800 brought surging faith in the efficacy of personal treatment in sheltered asylum environments. In England, such doctors as Thomas Arnold, Joseph Mason Cox, and Francis Willis (called in to treat George III in 1788) followed Battie's watchword that 'management did more than medicine' and pioneered a 'moral management' through which the experienced therapist would outwit the deluded psyche of his patient. A visitor was impressed by the tone of Willis's Lincolnshire madhouse:

> all the surrounding ploughmen, gardeners, threshers, thatchers, and other labourers, attired in black coats, white waistcoats, black silk breeches and stockings, and the head of each *bien poudrée, frisée*, and *arrangée*. These were the doctor's patients; and dress, neatness of person and exercise being the principal features of his admirable system, health and cheerfulness conjoined toward the recovery of every person attached to that most valuable asylum.

Summoned to treat his royal patient, Willis deployed a mix of psychological bullying, morale boosting, and fixing with the eye (to obtain dominance), all supplemented by such routine medication as blistering. George improved, to the nation's relief, although today his recovery is attributed to the natural remission of the acute intermittent porphyria (an inherited metabolic disorder, causing chronic pain and delirium) from which it is believed the monarch was suffering.

Shortly afterwards, the York Retreat developed 'moral therapy', with its emphasis upon community life in a domestic environment designed to recondition behaviour. The York Asylum, a charitable institution, had become bemired in scandal. By way of a counter-initiative, the local Quaker community, led by a tea merchant, William Tuke, established an alternative, the Retreat, opened in 1796. It was modelled on the ideal of bourgeois family life, and restraint was minimized. Patients and staff lived, worked, and dined together in an environment where recovery was encouraged through praise and blame, rewards and punishment, the goal being the restoration of self-control. In his *Description of the Retreat* (1813), Tuke's grandson Samuel noted that medical therapies had initially been tried there with little success; the Retreat had then abandoned 'medical' for 'moral' means, kindness, mildness, reason, and humanity, all within a family atmosphere—and with excellent results.

Comparable developments occurred elsewhere. In late-Enlightenment Florence, Dr Vicenzo Chiarugi (further discussed in Chapter 6) repudiated custodialism, medication, and restraint, and promoted therapies which treated the mad as human beings—'it is a supreme moral duty and medical obligation to respect the insane individual as a person.' Most highly publicized, however, were the reforms initiated at the Salpêtrière and Bicêtre Hospitals in Paris by Dr Philippe Pinel. Inspired by the Revolutionary ideals of liberty, equality, and fraternity, in 1793 Pinel figuratively (and perhaps literally) struck off the chains from his charges.

Pinel embraced the progressive thinking of the Enlightenment. If insanity was a mental disorder, it had to be relieved through mental approaches. Physical restraint was at best an irrelevance, at worst a lazy expedient and an irritant. Treatment must penetrate to the psyche.

During the Reign of Terror, a Parisian tailor challenged the execution of Louis XVI. Misconstruing a conversation he overheard, he then became convinced he was himself about to be guillotined. This delusion grew into a fixation necessitating his confinement. By way of psychotherapy, Pinel staged a complicated demonstration: three doctors, dressed up as magistrates, appeared before the tailor. Pretending to represent the revolutionary legislature, the panel pronounced his patriotism to be beyond reproach, 'acquitting' him of any misdeeds. The mock trial, Pinel noted, caused the man's symptoms to disappear at once.

Moral reformers like the Tukes and Pinel viewed madness as a breakdown of internal, rational discipline on the part of the sufferer. Their moral and psychological faculties needed to be rekindled, so that external coercion could be supplanted by inner

17 Philippe Pinel (1745–1826) pioneered moral therapy in revolutionary Paris and supposedly struck off the chains from the lunatics at the Salpêtrière and Bicêtre asylums; engraving after Mme Mérimée, 1810.

self-control. Psychiatry must reanimate reason or conscience. For this the closed environment of the asylum was tailor-made.

These reformist ideals chimed with the socio-political optimism of the revolutionary era. Progressives wished to sweep away the relics of the *ancien régime* madhouse. As citadels of repression, mindless coercion, and hopeless confinement, benighted bastilles like Bethlem must be purged. A House of Commons committee heard that one patient there, James Norris, had been shockingly restrained for many years:

> a stout iron ring was riveted round his neck, from which a short chain passed through a ring made to slide upwards and downwards on an upright massive iron bar, more than six feet high, inserted into the wall. Round his body a strong iron bar about two inches wide was riveted; on each side of the bar was a circular projection; which being fashioned to and enclosing each of his arms, pinioned them close to his sides.

Bethlem's physician Thomas Monro lamely reassured the Committee that such gothic fetters were 'fit only for the pauper lunatics: if a gentleman was put in irons he would not like it'. Tuke's *Description* offered, by contrast, a shining model for reform. As with Pinel, moral therapy was justified in England on the twin grounds of humanity and efficacy.

The idealized asylum

Criticism thus led not to the abolition of the madhouse, but to its rebirth, and institutionalization was transformed from a hand-to-mouth expedient into a positive ideal. In France the reforms of Pinel and the new legal requirements of the Napoleonic Code were further codified in the key statute of 1838. This formally required each *département* either to establish public asylums, or to ensure the provision of adequate facilities. It guarded against improper confinement by establishing rules for the certification of lunatics by medical officers—though for paupers a prefect's signature remained sufficient. Prefects were also given powers to inspect. Similar legislation was passed in Belgium twelve years later.

A comparable reform programme was put through in England, despite opposition from vested medical interests. Scandals revealing the improper confinement of the *sane* had already led to the Madhouses Act of 1774. Under its provisions, private madhouses had to be licensed annually by magistrates; a maximum size for each asylum was established; renewal of licences would depend upon satisfactory maintenance of admissions registers. Magistrates were empowered to carry out visitations (in London the inspecting body was a committee of the Royal College of Physicians). Most importantly, certification was instituted. Henceforth, although paupers could continue to be confined by magistrates, for all others a letter from a medical practitioner would be required to make confinement lawful.

Further reforms followed. The 1774 legislation was strengthened in a series of Acts passed from 1828, above all establishing the Commissioners in Lunacy, first for the metropolis and then for the whole country. The Commissioners constituted a permanent body of inspectors (made up of doctors and lawyers) empowered to prosecute unlawful practices and to deny renewal of licences. They also took it upon themselves to improve and standardize care and treatment. The Commission ensured eradication of the worst abuses, for example, by requiring that all cases of the use of restraint should be documented.

Safeguards against improper confinement were extended. Under an influential consolidating Act of 1890, *two* medical certificates were required for the detention of *all* patients. In the long run, these legalistic scruples may have proved a mixed blessing. For by insisting that only formally certified lunatics be detained in an asylum, it delayed its transformation into a more 'open' institution, easier of access and exit. Rather it was confirmed as a closed location of last resort, and certification became associated with protracted detention. The result was a failure to provide institutional care tailored for the temporarily or partially disturbed, and to isolate the asylum from the community.

Similar developments occurred in the United States, where the asylum arrived in the nineteenth century. The success of the York Retreat was the impulse behind the Frankford Asylum in Pennsylvania (1817), the Friends' Asylum near Philadelphia (1817), the McClean Hospital in Boston (1818), the Bloomingdale Asylum in New York (1821), and the Hartford Retreat in Hartford, Connecticut, founded in 1824. Most early American asylums combined private (paying) and public (charity) patients. As in France, the early asylum era in America was spearheaded by physicians specializing in mental disorders, notably Samuel B. Woodward at the Worcester State Hospital and Pliny Earle of the Bloomingdale Asylum in New York, both of whom integrated medical and moral therapies in a climate of Pinelian therapeutic optimism. They were among the thirteen originators of the Association of Medical

18 Lunatic Asylum, New York. In the nineteenth century it became customary to build lunatic asylums in the countryside, since it was believed that natural surroundings had healing properties.

Superintendents of American Institutions for the Insane, established in 1844—it later became the American Psychiatric Association.

The asylum as panacea

Throughout Europe, it was the nineteenth century which brought a skyrocketing in the number and scale of mental hospitals. In England, patient numbers climbed from perhaps 10,000 in 1800 to ten times that number in 1900. The jump in numbers was especially marked in new nation states. In Italy, no more than 8,000 had been confined as late as 1881; by 1907 that had soared to 40,000.

Such increases are not hard to explain. Positivistic, bureaucratic, utilitarian, and professional mentalities vested great faith in institutional solutions in general—indeed quite literally in bricks and mortar. Schools, workhouses, prisons, hospitals, and asylums—would these not contain and solve the social problems spawned by demographic change, urbanization, and industrialization?

Keen attention was paid to fine-tuning the asylum and many innovations were pioneered. In England 'non-restraint' was introduced in the 1830s, by Robert

19 The Lincoln Asylum was partly private and partly charitable. It achieved fame as the institution in which non-restraint therapies were pioneered in the 1830s by Robert Gardiner Hill.

Gardiner Hill at the Lincoln Asylum and independently John Conolly at the new Middlesex County Lunatic Asylum at Hanwell on London's western outskirts. Taking moral therapy to its logical conclusion, Hill and Conolly renounced all forms of mechanical coercion whatsoever: not just irons and manacles but fabric cuffs and straitjackets too. These would be replaced by surveillance under ample trained attendants and a regime of labour, which would stimulate the mind and discipline the body. 'In all cases of mental disorder', wrote Conolly, 'the regular life led by patients in asylums is to a great extent remedial.' Hill demonstrated his impressive success at Lincoln, as shown in the table (p. 115).

Numbers spoke volumes, but Gardiner Hill also answered his critics:

> But, it may be demanded, 'What mode of treatment do you adopt, in place of restraint? How do you guard against accidents?' In short, what is the substitute for coercion? The answer may be summed up in a few words, viz,—classification—vigilant and unceasing attendance by day and by night—kindness, occupation, and attention to health, cleanliness, and comfort, and the total absence of every description of other occupation of the attendant. This treatment in a properly constructed and suitable building, with a sufficient number of strong and active attendants always at their post, is

Year	Total number of Patients in the House	Total number of Patients Restrained	Total number of Instances of Restraint	Total number of Hours passed under Restraint
1829	72	39	1,727	29,424
1830	92	54	2,364	27,113¾
1831	70	40	1,004	10,830
1832	81	55	1,401	15,671½
1833	87	44	1,109	12,003½
1834	109	45	647	6,597
1835	108	28	323	2,874
1836	115	12	39	334
1837	130	2	3	28
1838	148	0	0	0

best calculated to restore the patient; and all instruments of coercion and torture are rendered absolutely and in every case unnecessary.

Despite Pinel's striking off of the chains, absolute non-restraint was seen by Continental reformers as a quixotically English *idée fixe*, a foible of doctrinaire liberalism, and it was little imitated. But French and German reformers made resourceful use of the asylum environment in their own ways. Work therapy was widely favoured. Planted in the countryside, the asylum typically became a self-sufficient colony, with its own farms, laundries, and workshops, partly for reasons of economy, partly to implement cures through labour. In France balneological treatments became a key feature of 'asylum science' (*police intérieure*). In Germany, C. F. W. Roller spelt out detailed directives for such matters as non-slip, smell-proof flooring, good drains, apparel, diet, and exercise at the influential Illenau asylum in Baden, where music and movement therapies were also pioneered. Everywhere, the care and cure of the mad became the subjects of the new 'science' of asylum management, spread by professional organs such as the significantly named *Asylum Journal*.

Architecture was held of cardinal importance. Expert design had to ensure maximum security, ample ventilation, efficient drainage, and optimal visibility along the lines of Benthamite panopticism, though few asylums were actually built specifically according to Jeremy Bentham's panopticon blueprint. Crucial was the classification of the different grades of lunatics: men had to be separated from women, incurables from curables, the violent from the harmless, the clean from the dirty; and a ladder of progress established so that the improving could ascend towards discharge. Meticulous classification became the first commandment of asylum managers. And all these aims had to be achieved compatibly with order, economy, efficiency, and discipline.

Asylums had never lacked critics: Bedlam was long a byword for man's inhumanity to man. A literature of patient protest gathered momentum in the eighteenth century, exposing brutality and neglect, and in the following century such campaigners as Louisa Lowe denounced 'the bastilles of England'. Radical undercurrents within the medical profession itself moreover insisted that, with the best will in the world, asylums must prove counter-productive 'manufactories of madness': herded together, lunatics would be reduced to the lowest common denominator. For long advocates outnumbered adversaries, however, and the asylum movement was buoyed up on waves of optimism. In 1837 Dr W. A. F. Browne, a pupil of Esquirol and head of the Montrose Royal Lunatic Asylum in Scotland, pronounced on *What Asylums Were, Are, and Ought to Be.* Traditional institutions had been abominations; present ones were better, and the asylum of the future would be positively paradisiacal:

Conceive a spacious building resembling the palace of a

peer, airy, and elevated, and elegant, surrounded by extensive and swelling grounds and gardens. The interior is fitted up with galleries, and workshops, and music-rooms. The sun and the air are allowed to enter at every window, the view of the shrubberies and fields, and groups of labourers, is unobstructed by shutters or bars; all is clean, quiet and attractive. The inmates all seem to be actuated by the common impulse of enjoyment, all are busy, and delighted by being so. The house and all around appears a hive of industry . . . There is in this community no compulsion, no chains, no whips, no corporal chastisement, simply because these are proved to be less effectual means of carrying any point than persuasion, emulation, and the desire of obtaining gratification. . . .

Such is a faithful picture of what may be seen in many institutions, and of what might be seen in all, were asylums conducted as they ought to be.

Many, like Browne, believed, or wanted to believe, that such institutions were entirely beneficent.

The asylum as problem

A new pessimism, however, made itself heard in the last third of the nineteenth century. Discharge figures showed that expectations that the asylum would become a panacea were grossly over-optimistic. Cure rates dipped as public asylums silted up with long-stay zombie-like patients.

To some extent, psychiatrists were victims of their own propaganda. They had insisted that many of the aberrant and antisocial behaviours traditionally labelled vice, sin, and crime were actually mental disorders in need of the doctor and the asylum. As a result, magistrates deflected difficult cases from the workhouse or jail, but superintendents then discovered to their dismay and cost that rehabilitation posed more problems than anticipated. Furthermore, the senile and the demented, along with epileptics, paralytics, sufferers from tertiary syphilis (GPI), and other degenerative neurological disorders were increasingly shepherded through the asylum gates. For all such conditions, the prognosis was gloomy, and the asylum became a dustbin for hopeless cases.

Psychiatry adapted in response. If 'moral therapy' did not work, did that not suggest that much insanity was, after all, chronic, indeed ingrained, constitutional, and probably hereditary? Investigation seemed to show that madness was passed down from generation to generation, that society harboured an 'iceberg' of atavistic degenerates and defectives. Confronted by these intractable problems, 'degenerationist' psychiatrists (discussed in Chapter 6) held there was little that could be done beyond shutting such threats away where they would at least be safe and prevented from breeding future generations of recidivists and imbeciles. The Irish inspectors of lunacy expressed this new pessimism as early as 1851, when they announced that 'the uniform tendency of all asylums is to degenerate from their original object, that of being hospitals for the treatment of insanity, into domiciles for incurable lunatics'.

In this climate, public asylums grew larger—the average English specimen housed 116 patients in 1827 but nearly ten times as many in 1910, while Colney Hatch Asylum in north London held over 3,000—but degenerated into sites dominated by formal drills, financial stringency, and drug routines (like bromides and chloral hydrate) meant to pacify, sedate, and stupefy. In the USA there was a slide from the optimism of moral therapy to a preoccupation with security and sedation. Quality of care declined. Set up in the first half of the nineteenth century, the Pennsylvania Asylum initially promoted high levels of community and family involvement, underpinned by a curative ideology. By the last decades of the century, however, a more organic psychiatry had become dominant, justifying the habitual use of sedatives and marking a decline in personal therapy.

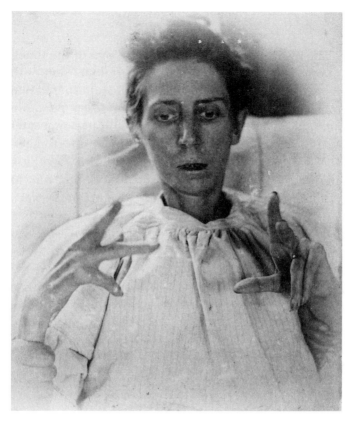

20 This late Victorian photograph from Colney Hatch Asylum shows a woman suffering from mania, with forearm, hand, and finger movements. Such photographs were widely used for teaching and diagnostic purposes. Colney Hatch opened in North London in July 1851. Initially it held 1,250 patients, but by the time it was renamed as Friern Hospital in 1937, it had been enlarged and held 2,700. The hospital closed in the 1990s.

The institutionalization drive was a sign of the times. It combined the imperatives of the rational state with the expedients of a market economy, and ushered in a progressive therapeutic optimism under a pervasive paternalism—the idea that social and professional elites have the right and responsibility to treat unfortunates. Not least, the asylum idea reflected the long-term cultural shift from religion to scientific secularism. In traditional Christendom, it was the distinction between believers and heretics, saints and sinners, which had been crucial—that between the sane and the crazy had counted for little. This changed, and the great divide, since the 'age of reason', became that between the rational and the rest, demarcated and enforced at bottom by the asylum walls. The keys of St Peter had been replaced by the keys of psychiatry. The instituting of the asylum set up a cordon sanitaire delineating the 'normal' from the 'mad', which underlined the Otherhood of the insane and carved out a managerial milieu in which that alienness could be handled.

6

The rise of psychiatry

Canst thou not minister to a mind diseased?
(*Macbeth*)

Mechanizing madness

Modern times inherited varied models of madness. Within Christendom, abnormality, as we have seen, had commonly been diagnosed as supernatural, be it diabolical or divine. Renaissance humanism and scientific rationalism by contrast advanced naturalistic and medical concepts. The mechanical philosophy's orderly law-governed universe discounted satanic possession, while mania and melancholy, insisted enlightened physicians, originated not in the skies but in the soma; the aetiology of insanity was organic.

But if so, precisely which organs and operations were

implicated? The old humoral readings of mental disorder, which had stressed the roles of blood and yellow bile ('choler') in mania and black bile in melancholia, lost credit amongst the medical community as the 'new science' refigured the body in mechanical terms which highlighted the solids (organs, nerves, and fibres) rather than the fluids. Iatrophysics (medical physics) pictured the body machine as a hydraulic system of piping, or as a neurological circuit wiring the limbs to the brain and conducting sensation and motion electrically.

One upshot was that in post-Cartesian medical writings 'mental illness' in the strict sense became almost a contradiction in terms: the possibility of the mind or spirit per se being diseased was programmatically ruled out. Within Cartesian and Newtonian frameworks, the soul became definitionally inviolable, and doctors instead referred insanity to lesions of the *body*.

Developing that line of thinking, the Oxford-educated London physician Thomas Willis (1621–75) coined the term neurology and elaborated Descartes' idea of the 'reflex'. An avid dissector, Willis strove to localize mental functions to particular regions of the brain. His models of the central and peripheral nervous system depended on the operations of animal spirits, superfine chemical intermediaries between body and mind capable of being affected by either.

Proceeding on similar lines were Archibald Pitcairn, a Scot who taught at Leiden in the Netherlands, and his protégé, Richard Mead. Lunatics, argued Mead, suffered from false ideas induced by the chaotic activities of those volatile animal spirits; these in turn fed back into the muscles to produce confused and uncontrolled movements in the limbs. The madman was thus a disordered sensory-motor machine in a state of breakdown—delirium, for instance, held Mead, was 'not a distemper of the mind but of the body'. Such somaticism served to confirm the authority of medicine, while also assuaging anxiety and stigma amongst patients, who would no longer be thought to be 'lost souls', clean 'out of their mind'.

The re-ascription of madness as, at bottom, a bodily disorder was systematized in the teachings of Herman Boerhaave. In true Cartesian manner, that highly influential Leiden professor and his many disciples, notably Albrecht von Haller, maintained that the essential symptoms of madness lay in beliefs which, though lacking objective existence, were mistaken for reality. These delusions had a physical source—melancholy for instance resulted from the 'dissipation' (evaporation) of the most volatile parts of the blood and the thickening of its 'black, fat and earthy' residue, causing lethargy. Friedrich Hoffmann, professor of medicine at Halle, already discussed in Chapter 2, developed a comparable solidist psychopathology based on the vessels, fibres, and pores.

With this somatic turn, the nervous system became the focal point of enquiry and explanation. Followers of Pitcairn, in particular his fellow Scot George Cheyne, speculated about the sympathy of the vascular and nervous systems with the brain. Imaging of the nerves as hollow pipes or as wires conveying waves or electrical impulses produced theories in which disordered thoughts and mood-swings were put down to some defect of the digestive and nervous systems, which led to slackness, excessive tension, or obstruction. The fervent Newtonian Nicholas Robinson maintained in his *A New System of the Spleen* (1729) that it was the nerve fibres which controlled behaviour; pathological laxity in them was the primary cause of melancholia. 'Every change of the Mind', he insisted, 'indicates a Change in the Bodily Organs.' Far from being a matter of malingering on the one hand or 'imaginary Whims and Fancies' on the other, insanity was thus a genuine malady, rooted in 'the real, mechanical Affections of Matter and Motion'.

In the New World, Benjamin Rush of Philadelphia, the physician officially acknowledged by the American Psychiatric Association as the 'father of American psychiatry', held that practically all mental disorders were due to vitiated blood. His systematic remedy was bloodletting.

The psychological turn

After 1750 a theoretical transformation came about, owing in part to the growing uptake of those philosophical theories of sensation and perception promoted by the empiricist philosopher John Locke and furthered by the *philosophe* Condillac. Replacing Cartesian innate ideas with a model of the mind as originally a blank sheet of paper, John Locke, as we have seen, had suggested in his *Essay on Human Understanding* (1690) that madness was due to faulty associations in the processes whereby sense data were transformed into 'ideas'. Lockean (mis)-association of ideas became central to new thinking about madness, above all in Britain but also in France.

Lockean thinking was then medicalized in part through William Cullen, doyen of the flourishing medical school set up in 1726 at Edinburgh University, who produced a more psychological paradigm of insanity. Basically imputing madness to excessive irritation of the nerves, Cullen held that the precipitating cause of derangement lay in acute cerebral activity. Insanity

THE RISE OF PSYCHIATRY

(*vesania*) was a nervous disorder, which arose when there was 'some inequality in the excitement of the brain', and he coined the term 'neurosis' to denote any illness consequent upon such a disorder of the nervous system (by Freud's day, of course, the meaning of 'neurosis' had utterly changed). Yet, within this somatic model, insanity was also for Cullen an 'unusual and commonly hurried association of ideas', leading to 'false judgement' and producing 'disproportionate emotions'—in other words, it was a *mental* disorder, albeit one grounded in dynamic neurophysiology. The psychological inspiration for this came from Cullen's friend, the philosopher David Hume, who held Lockean sense impressions and associations of ideas fundamental to all intellectual operations. Cullen's importance thus lay in reintegrating the mental into medical discourses on madness. His teachings proved highly influential.

The break with earlier (Boerhaavian) somatic theories of madness was clear by 1780. In his *Observations on the Nature, Kinds, Causes and Prevention of Insanity, Lunacy or Madness* (1782–86), Thomas Arnold, who had studied under Cullen before taking over a Leicester madhouse, constructed a nosology (taxonomy) of insanity on the basis of the Lockean philosophy of mind, distinguishing 'ideal insanity' (hallucination) from 'notional insanity' (delusion). Acknowledging his debt to 'our British Psychologists, such as Locke, Hartley, Reid, Priestley, Stewart, Kames', Alexander Crichton's *An Inquiry into the Nature and Origin of Mental Derangement* (1798) similarly argued that psychiatry should be based on the philosophy of mind.

This emerging model of madness as a psychological condition pointed to an alternative target for psychiatric enquiry: rather than the organs of the body, the doctor had to address the patient's psyche, as evidenced by his behaviour. The case-history approach this entailed demanded the transformation of the old craft of minding the insane into the pursuit of systematic psychological observation. The years after 1770 brought a spurt in psychiatric publishing along these lines by owners of private madhouses, for instance William Perfect's *Methods of Cure, in Some Particular Cases of Insanity* (1778). Initially such houses had been rather secretive, but this changed, as new thinking demanded and prized the observation of individual patients and the publicization of findings. The handling by Francis Willis of George III's first bout of madness (1788–9) similarly highlighted the psychological—and the recovery of the 'mad king' bred optimism.

The close of the century brought a remarkable marriage across enlightened Europe between new psychological thinking and reformist practice in what has been called 'moral therapy'. Its leading British exponent, the York Retreat, has already been discussed in Chapter 5. Another pioneer was the Florentine physician, Vincenzo Chiarugi, encouraged by the reforming activities of the enlightened Grand Duke of Tuscany, Peter Leopold. Expounded in *On Insanity* (1793–4), a major three-volume text, Chiarugi's medico-psychiatric theories held that bodily states influenced the mind via the activities of the senses and the nervous system at large. His notion that the 'sensorium commune' mediated between the intellect and the senses, between soul and body, offered a psycho-physiological solution to the old Cartesian problem of mind/body dualism. Pondering the aetiology of insanity, Chiarugi backed the Enlightenment view that mental conditions were acquired rather than inherited, and held out high hopes for cure, not primarily by medical means but through humane management. Repudiating the use of force, he touted the superior efficacy of 'moral control', a therapy of psychological ascendancy over the patient established by the physician through character, expertise, and moral example.

In Paris the physician Philippe Pinel pioneered similar psychological approaches at the Bicêtre, the main public madhouse for men, and the Salpêtrière, its

21 The Florentine physician, Vincenzo Chiarugi (1759–1820) introduced moral treatment into Italy; engraving by de Lasimo, 1804.

female counterpart. His stress on psychogenic factors rested upon enlightened foundations: empirical observation failed to discern any underlying structural abnormalities in lunatics' brains when examined post mortem. Moreover, philosophically, Pinel was an *idéologue*, influenced by Locke's thinking as radicalized by Condillac. Contrary to Locke, however, his *traitement moral* was directed to the affective, as opposed to the intellectual, side of the psyche.

Whilst retaining the traditional division of insanity into melancholia, mania, idiocy, and dementia, Pinel also developed new disease categories. His *manie sans délire*, later called *folie raisonnante*, outlined a partial insanity: sufferers would be mad on one subject alone. While the understanding remained sound, the personality was warped. Like other moral therapists, Pinel was an optimist: truly organic brain disease might be incurable, but functional disorders like melancholy and 'mania without delirium' were responsive to psychological methods. His *Medico-philosophical Treatise on Mental Alienation or Mania* (1801), which set out his thinking on the moral causation and treatment of insanity, was translated into English, Spanish, and German and proved highly influential.

22 Eight women representing the conditions of dementia, megalomania, acute mania, melancholia, idiocy, hallucination, erotic mania, and paralysis, in the gardens of the Salpêtrière Hospital, Paris; lithograph by A. Gautier, 1857.

Psychiatry French-style

Pinel's favourite follower was Jean-Etienne Dominique Esquirol (1772–1840), whose *Mental Maladies* (1838) was the outstanding psychiatric text of his age. While asserting the ultimately organic nature of psychiatric disorders, Esquirol concentrated, like his mentor, on their psycho-social triggers. The diagnosis of 'mono-mania' was developed to describe a partial insanity identified with affective disorders, especially those involving paranoia, and he further delineated such conditions as kleptomania, nymphomania, and pyro-mania, detectable in advance only to the trained eye. A champion of the asylum as a therapeutic instrument, he became an authority on its design, and planned the National Asylum at Charenton, a suburb of Paris, of which he was appointed director. (It briefly housed the ageing Marquis de Sade.)

Translating into psychiatric practice the commitment of French hospital medicine at large to close clinical observation, Esquirol developed influential accounts, derived from extensive case experience, of illusion, hal-lucination, and moral insanity. He also trained up the next cohort of French psychiatrists, who then went on to plough furrows of their own: E. E. Georget wrote on cerebral localization; Louis Calmeil described dementia paralytica; J. J. Moreau de Tours was, as we shall see, a pioneer of degenerationism; while Jean-Pierre Falret and Jules Baillarger offered rival but complementary accounts of the manic-depressive cycle (the former called it *folie circulaire*, the latter *folie à double forme*).

Esquirol's transformation of the classification and diagnosis of mental disorder was made possible by the abundance of data provided by asylums, enabling diagnosticians to build up clearly defined profiles of psychiatric diseases capable of being identified by their symptoms. Observation of asylum patients led to more precise differentiations in theory and practice—epileptics, for instance, became standardly distinguished from the insane. Esquirol himself produced an improved description of *petit mal*, and his pupil Calmeil described 'absence', distinguishing between passing mental confusion and the onset of a *grand mal* attack. Esquirol organized a special hospital for epileptics; by 1860, such institutions had also been founded in Britain and Germany, and in 1891 the first US hospital was established in Gallipolis, Ohio.

Similarly, the condition known as general paresis of the insane (one manifestation of tertiary syphilis) was elucidated in 1822 by Antoine Laurent Bayle. Although the micro-organism which causes syphilis had not yet been discovered—the bacteriological era lay ahead—

the neurological and psychological features of GPI (notably euphoria and expansiveness), combined with the organic changes revealed by autopsy, supported Esquirol's conviction that psychiatric disorders could be revealed using the techniques championed by such great French pathological anatomists as Laennec who had investigated tuberculosis and other internal conditions.

Closely related to GPI, *tabes dorsalis* was another disorder, prevalent in the nineteenth century, which became the focus of neuro-pathological research. It was the subject of a masterly clinical study published in 1858 by Guillaume Duchenne, which established its syphilitic origin: so definitive was his account that it was soon named 'Duchenne's disease'. He was also at the forefront in describing many other neurological disorders involving personality degeneration, including progressive muscular atrophy and locomotor ataxia (lack of coordination in movement).

Duchenne's contemporary, Jean-Martin Charcot (1825–93), Clinical Professor of the Nervous System at the Salpêtrière, was the most famous teacher of the *belle époque,* and his clinic became the neurologists' and psychiatrists' Mecca (Freud studied under him there). His *Lectures on Nervous Diseases Delivered at the Salpêtrière* (1872–87) brought order to the nosology of those kinds of neurological disorders which shaded into the domain of psychiatry.

Charcot was never an 'alienist' (asylum superintendent) in the tradition of Pinel and Esquirol, and, contrary to a popular image, he was by no means exclusively preoccupied with hysteria. He was, first and foremost, a passionate neurologist (hence his soubriquet, the 'Napoleon of the neuroses'), committed to deploying patho-anatomical techniques, so as to bring order to the chaos of neurological symptom clusters.

Conditions like epilepsy, general paralysis, and *tabes dorsalis,* he granted, 'come to us like so many Sphinxes', defying 'the most penetrating anatomical investigations'. Aspiring to trace their bizarre symptoms to organic lesions, he undertook a massive clinical scrutiny of abnormalities: tics, migraine, epileptiform seizures, aphasia (language and speech disorders), mutism, somnambulism, hallucinations, contractures, and other deficits. Clinical observation, he was confident, would lay bare the natural histories of, and the laws governing, extended families of related neuro-psychological conditions: chorea, St Vitus' Dance, sclerosis, tertiary neurosyphilitic infections, temporal lobe epilepsy, and a multitude of other neuropathies. 'These diseases', he insisted, 'do not form, in pathology, a class apart, governed by other physiological laws than the common

23 A high-profile neurologist and psychiatrist, Jean-Martin Charcot (1825–93) gained greatest public prominence for his theatrical demonstrations of hysteria.

ones.' One valuable part of this project was his further development of James Parkinson's early work on the 'shaking palsy'—indeed it was Charcot who first called it 'Parkinson's disease'.

Charcot similarly insisted that hysteria was no impenetrable mystery, but, like any other neurological disorder, was marked by definite, law-governed, predictable, clinical manifestations. With unlimited access to clinical material at his Salpêtrière base, he mobilized a research industry and played a key, but ambivalent, role in the emergence of modern psychiatry.

Psychiatry German-style

The principalities which made up pre-unification Germany developed renowned asylums of their own, notably the Illenau in Baden-Baden, where Richard von Krafft-Ebing (1840–1902), pioneer of sexual psychiatry, gained his early clinical experience. Unlike in France or Britain, however, German psychiatry was chiefly associated with the universities and their research mentality. Perhaps for that reason, German-speaking psychiatry became the battleground for fierce theoretical controversies between rival organic and psychological camps.

At the turn of the nineteenth century Johann Christian Reil (who coined the word 'Psychiaterie') developed a holistic approach, indebted to Romanticism's preoccupation with the irrational depths of the psyche. While, as a physician, tracing madness to the nerves and brain, his psychodynamically oriented *Rhapsodies on the Use of Psychological Treatment Methods in Mental Breakdown* (1803) proposed an idiosyncratic variant on moral treatment: the charismatic alienist would master the delinquent mind; a staff trained in play-acting would further the alienist's efforts to break the patient's fixed ideas—and all would be combined with salutary doses of therapeutic terror (sealing-wax dropped onto the palms, immersion in a tub of eels, etc.).

Psychological approaches were further developed by J. C. A. Heinroth and Karl Ideler, who drew heavily on Romanticism's metaphysical plumbing of the inner consciousness. A Lutheran Pietist who taught at Leipzig, Heinroth viewed mental disorder in religious terms, and the aetiological explanations offered in his *Textbook of Mental Disturbances* (1818) was dismissive of the idea of physical causation: 'in the great majority of cases', he insisted, 'it is not the body but the soul itself from which mental disturbances directly and primarily originate.'

Heinroth linked insanity with sin; both were voluntary and hence culpable renunciations of God's gift, free will. Moral treatment must expose the lunatic to the healthy and devout personality of the alienist. Rather as for Reil, gentle therapies were to be combined with severe shock, restraint, and punishments. Each case required individual diagnosis and treatment. Eventually the patient would recover self-command.

Slightly later, the Viennese physician Ernst von Feuchtersleben (1806–49) aimed to integrate both psychic and somatic strands into a personality-based psychiatry offered as an ambitious synthesis of neurophysiology, psychology, and psychotherapeutics. Developing something akin to the modern concept of 'psychosis', he construed 'psychopathy' as a disease of the whole personality.

Other German and Austrian psychiatrists, by contrast, denounced the speculative fantasies of 'psychicists' like Heinroth, which they associated with the maunderings of speculative Romantic anti-science, and turned in an organic direction. Setting the cat amongst the pigeons in the debate on the nature and causes of insanity was phrenology, a would-be science developed by the Vienna-trained anatomists Franz Joseph Gall (1758–1828) and J. C. Spurzheim (1776–1832). Phrenology controversially maintained that the seat of the mind was the brain, whose configurations both determined and displayed the personality. The brain

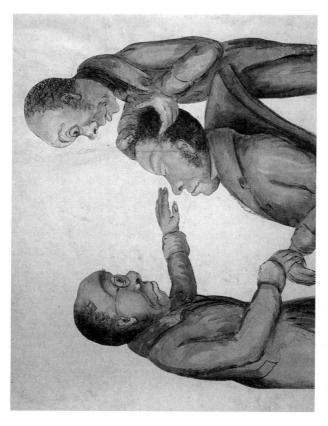

24 Franz Joseph Gall and Johann Caspar Spurzheim, the founders of phrenology, are shown examining a patient by feeling the bumps on his head; watercolour painting, early nineteenth century.

itself was an ensemble of over thirty separate 'organs' (acquisitiveness, sexuality, piety, and so forth), each occupying a specific cortical area. An organ's size governed the power of its operations; the contours of the skull flagged the lineaments of the brain beneath, while the overall topography (hills and valleys) of the 'bumps' determined personality.

Pious critics condemned phrenology for being materialistic, and Gall, a talented anatomist, was hounded out of Vienna in 1805. Nevertheless, it gained international attention, amongst doctors and the general public alike, because it seemed an aid to self-understanding; and it appealed to many alienists, since it posited a real biomedical basis for mental disturbance. Phrenological or not, 'medical materialism' of various stripes—the idea of a physical substrate to insanity—buttressed the doctors' claim that psychiatric practice should be exclusive to the medically qualified, sanctioned laboratory research and gave some credibility to the ragbag of physical treatments, notably sedatives, bathing, purging, and bleeding, which formed the stock-in-trade of the profession.

Amongst German somatists, Maximilian Jacobi (1775–1858) was the pioneer, and the main aetiological assumptions were then laid down in J. B. Friedreich's *Attempt at a History of the Literature of the Pathology and Therapy of Psychic Illnesses* (1830). Somatic psychiatry was given its chief impetus, orientation, and authority, however, by Wilhelm Griesinger, professor at Berlin. Enthusiastic in his championing of the materialism underpinning the experimental electro-physiologies of Helmholtz and du Bois-Reymond, Griesinger boldly asserted in his *Pathology and Therapy of Psychiatric Diseases* (1845) that 'mental illnesses are brain diseases'. His sound bite that 'every mental disease is rooted in brain disease' inspired research into brain pathology aimed at discovering the precise cortical location of mental illnesses. Commitment to the somatic origin of such disorders spurred scientific investigation, while also, perhaps, restoring dignity to patients stigmatized by the lunacy diagnosis. For Griesinger it was crucially important that study of mental illness should not isolate itself from general medicine but be integral to it: an oft-repeated cry in the chequered history of psychiatry.

Mental diseases, Griesinger believed, were typically progressive, worsening from depressive states into more disruptive conditions. This reflected a pattern of underlying somatic abnormality, which would begin with excessive cerebral irritation, lead to chronic, irreversible brain degeneration, and end in the disintegration of the ego common in dementia. This stress upon the longitudinal descent from normal to pathological psychic processes, and on the progressive path of psychiatric illnesses, was later taken up by Kraepelin.

Griesinger set the mould for German academic psychiatry, in particular through his call for the alliance of psychiatry and neurology in academic neuropsychiatric clinics. After 1850, university psychiatry prospered in the German-speaking lands, supported by those twin pillars which gave German medical education its prestige, the polyclinic and the research institute. Unlike asylum superintendents in England or the USA, top-flight university psychiatrists rarely shared their patients' lives night and day, and their orientation was theoretical and investigative rather than bureaucratic and therapeutic. University psychiatry's primary goal was the scientific understanding of disorders through systematic observation, experimentation, and dissection.

Following Griesinger, his Berlin successor Carl Westphal, and then Theodor Meynert, Carl Wernicke and their co-workers promoted a hard-nosed psychiatry, rooted in prestigious scientific materialism and wedded to histology, neurology, and neuropathology. Much specialized knowledge came to light from their systematic investigations—for instance 'Westphal's sign', the loss of the knee-jerk reflex in neurological disease.

A product of its illustrious medical school, Theodor

Meynert (1833–92) spent his entire career in Vienna, from 1870 as professor of psychiatry. Essentially a neuropathologist, drawing heavily upon microscopical techniques, he subtitled his textbook *A Clinical Treatise on the Diseases of the Forebrain* (1884) in protest against the wishy-washy mentalistic implications of 'psychiatry'. It was axiomatic for Meynert that each stimulus that reached the central nervous system excited a corresponding area in the cortex of the brain; he succeeded in demonstrating certain pathways by which cortical cells communicate with one another and with deeper cells of the cerebrum; and he advanced a systematic classification of mental illness based on his histopathological studies. Theoretically the bluntest of somatists, in practice, however, when his organic neuroanatomical programme ran into grave problems, he was reduced to devising some rather nebulous entities, such as the primary and secondary ego, to describe behavioural and cognitive disorders.

Carl Wernicke (1848–1905), one of Meynert's pupils, represents German neuropsychiatry at its apogee. His lifelong pursuit of cerebral localization (mapping which regions of the cerebral cortex are responsible for which functions) centred on a consuming interest in aphasia (language and speech disorders). Wernicke found that when patients had strokes in the posterior perisylvian part of the brain, they lost the ability to understand the spoken word or to speak intelligibly. This became known as 'Wernicke's aphasia', and the area of the brain 'Wernicke's area'. In his extremely influential three-volume *Manual of Brain Diseases* (1881–3), Wernicke attempted to ground psychiatric symptoms in brain abnormalities, and in particular lent his authority to the concept of cerebral dominance.

Degenerationism

The German somatists staked bold claims for science's capacity, through slicing up brains under microscopes in the lab or performing animal experiments, to provide explanations for the patho-physiological and neurological mechanisms of psychiatric disorders: functions could be mapped onto structures and their lesions. But they were far from sanguine about cures—and they were unashamedly more interested in diseases than in patients. This pessimism was in part a product of the inmate populations they saw, for asylums everywhere were filling up with those blighted with intractable and irreversible organic diseases, classically GPI (tertiary syphilis). Therapeutic nihilism born of experience bred a new hereditarianism. Pinel and other advocates of moral therapy and asylum reform had hailed the effectiveness of early treatment and environmental manipulation; by the *fin de siècle*, however, the build-up of long-stay cases was blighting hopes, and scrutiny of family backgrounds was pointing to inherited psychopathic taints. Such reflections were systematized into a degenerationist model by two psychiatrists, Esquirol's pupil J. Moreau de Tours and Bénédict Augustin Morel, and in England by the gloomy genius Henry Maudsley, who, while embracing Darwinian evolution, was principally haunted by the survival of the unfit in modern society.

Physician to two large asylums, Morel turned degeneration into an influential explanatory principle in his *Treatise on Physical and Moral Degeneration* (1857). Produced conjointly by organic and social factors, hereditary degeneration was said to be cumulative over the generations, descending into imbecility and, finally and thankfully, sterility. A degenerate's family history might sink, over the generations, from neurasthenia or nervous hysteria, through alcohol and opiate addiction, prostitution and criminality, to insanity proper and utter idiocy. Once a family was on the downhill slope, the outcome was hopeless.

Alcoholism—a concept coined in 1852 by the Swede Magnus Huss—provided a model for degeneration, since it combined the physical and the moral, was rife among pauper lunatics, and supposedly led to character disintegration. Valentin Magnan (1835–1916) implanted Morel's theories into evolutionary biology with his idea of 'progress or perish'; and such views were dramatized in Emile Zola's naturalistic novel *L'Assommoir* (1877), in which Magnan himself appears as an asylum doctor. Degenerationism caught the mood of the times in a France reeling from defeat by Prussia in the war of 1870, and from the subsequent and bloody Paris Commune; it also echoed bourgeois fears of a mass society marked by proletarian unrest and socialism.

Griesinger himself acknowledged his debt to Morel, while Meynert, Wernicke, and other brain psychiatrists further documented the hereditarian dimensions of insanity. Meynert's successor in Vienna, Richard von Krafft-Ebing, was a qualified exponent of degenerationist thinking. Best known for his *Psychopathia Sexualis* (1886), the founding study of sexual 'perversion' (bestiality, exhibitionism, fetishism, sado-masochism, transvestism, and so forth) and 'inversion' (that is, homosexuality), he classed such sexual conditions and various other disorders as constitutional degeneration.

Paul Möbius (1854–1907) also espoused degenerationism. Exploring the presumed connections between

25 The Vienna-based psychiatrist Richard von Krafft-Ebing (1845–1902) largely owed his fame to his studies of sexual perversion and psychopathology; photogravure, *c.*1900.

genius and insanity (see Chapter 4), Möbius focused on *dégénérés supérieurs*, i.e. individuals of abnormal aptitude. A particularly blatant misogynist in a profession which widely disparaged women's mental powers, he was also intrigued by hysteria and pathological sexuality: women were slaves to their bodies, he declared in his *The Physiological Feeble-Mindedness of Women* (1900)—'instinct makes the female animal-like'—and high intelligence in the sex was so singular as to be positively degenerate. Möbius also endorsed the notion of hereditary degeneration in a classification of psychiatric disorders admired by Emil Kraepelin.

Morelian ideas were taken up in Italy by the psychiatrist and criminologist Cesare Lombroso (1836–1909), who viewed criminals and psychiatric patients as degenerate throwbacks, identifiable by physical stigmata—low brows, jutting jaws, and so forth. Comparable physical evidence of degenerative taints could also be found in non-European races, in apes, and in children.

A more optimistic reading of similar tendencies was taken, predictably enough, in the new world, where George M. Beard (1839–83) popularized the concept of 'neurasthenia', nervous breakdown produced by the frantic pressures of advanced civilization, which drained the individual's reserves of 'nerve force'.

'*American nervousness is the product of American civilization*', he pronounced with mingled pride and regret. Neurasthenia's prevalence in the modern era was no mystery, held Beard: the telegraph, railroad, press, and the market-driven rat race of Wall Street had rendered life insupportably hectic, intense, and stressful. Civilization made demands on nervous systems that nature had never anticipated. As with the eighteenth-century 'English malady', neurasthenia struck the elite and flagged up civilization and its discontents. Beard's ideas were given a practical twist by Silas Weir Mitchell, who introduced the 'Weir Mitchell treatment'—bed rest, strict isolation, fattening up with milk puddings, and passive massage—to counter such fatiguing tendencies amongst the neurasthenic.

But American thinking had its darker side too. The trial in 1881 of Charles Guiteau, the assassin of President Garfield, spotlighted issues of heredity, criminality, and moral insanity, since psychiatrists based their defence testimonies on the claim that Guiteau was a degenerate. By 1900 lobbies were urging compulsory confinement, sterilization, and other eugenic measures, as well as the use of psychiatry in immigration control. Psychiatric sterilization gained a hold in the United States long before Nazi Germany.

The neurasthenia diagnosis was also exported to

Europe. In the Netherlands and Germany it tended to be integrated into the neuroses at large. In France Pierre Janet outlined a variant of his own known as psychasthenia. In Britain it seems to have made less headway because of continuing phlegmatic Anglo-Saxon resistance to pandering to psychic weakness.

Psychiatry and society

In all the advanced nations, psychiatry gained a public face (if little prestige and much distrust) after 1800, and psychiatrists found public employment in universities, especially in Germany, and in asylums. It came of professional age around the mid-century, when medical superintendents ('alienists') banded together to form specialized organizations. In England identity was consolidated in 1841 with the forming of the Association of Medical Officers of Asylums and Hospitals for the Insane, which published the *Asylum Journal* (1853), later renamed the *Journal of Mental Science* (1858). In due course it became the (Royal) Medico-Psychological Association, and finally in 1971 the Royal College of Psychiatrists. For its part, the forerunner of the American Psychiatric Association began in 1844 as the Association of Medical Superintendents of American

Institutions for the Insane. Professional journals widely emerged, like the *Annales médico-psychologiques* in France and the *Archiv für Psychiatrie*, set up by Griesinger.

Psychiatrists inevitably played a growing role in the public domain, notably in the courtroom. Lunatics and 'idiots' had long been, under certain circumstances, made wards of the state, and it was accepted that the insane, not being responsible for their acts, should be exempt from punishment for criminal deeds. In 1799, for example, when James Hadfield tried to assassinate George III, the trial was halted once his lawyer convinced the court that the accused was besieged by religious delusions. (He had grown convinced that only by his death could the world be saved, and that he was sure to be executed for killing the king.) Thereafter juries in England could formally bring in verdicts of 'not guilty by reason of insanity', and the accused would be put under psychiatric lock and key.

Telling criminality from insanity had never been thought to require medical expertise: friends and family had been called in to testify in court. This changed from the early decades of the nineteenth century, however, when psychiatric experts staked out new claims to detect 'partial' insanity, particularly the Esquirolian monomanias, imperceptible to the untrained eye.

The insanity plea became controversial in Britain

when the trial in 1843 of Daniel M'Naghten for the murder of Prime Minister Sir Robert Peel's private secretary was stopped on the grounds of insanity. The resulting furore led to new guidelines being drawn up, by the House of Lords, to clarify the legal basis for criminal insanity. The M'Naghten Rules (1844) grounded the insanity defence in the defendant's inability to distinguish right from wrong. This pre-empted the claim advanced by post-Esquirolian psychiatrists that the grounds should be 'irresistible impulse', that is, disorders of emotion and volition, independently of delusions of the understanding. In France by contrast, 'irresistible impulse' and partial and temporary insanity figured large in the plea of insanity and *crime passionelle*. Disputes over the insanity defence (who was bad? who was mad?) highlighted conflicts between legal and psychiatric models of the person, and left the public standing of psychiatry dubious.

The mad

A dialogue of the deaf?

'One half of mankind does not know how the other half lives,' opens the autobiography of an early twentieth-century British mental patient who signed himself 'Warmark'. The rich may not understand the poor, nor atheists the God-fearing, but the experience most profoundly closed, 'Warmark' suggested, is surely being out of your mind. So can the utterances of the insane make sense?

Some experts say no: the language of the mentally ill is an irredeemable babble. Psychiatry had taken a wrong turn, argued the distinguished British psychiatrists Richard Hunter and Ida Macalpine in 1974, when they wrote,

> Today, it is assumed that mental pathology derives from normal psychology and can be understood in terms of faulty inter or intrapersonal relationships and corrected

by re-education or psychoanalysis of where the patient's emotional development went wrong. Despite all efforts which have gone into this approach and all the reams devoted to it, results have been meagre not to say inconclusive, and contrast sharply with what medicine has given to psychiatry and which is added to year by year. [This is because] Patients are victims of their brain rather than their mind. To reap the rewards of this medical approach, however, means a reorientation of psychiatry, from listening to looking.

It is surely significant that when they undertook a full-length study of the madness of King George III, they chose not to read any psychiatric significance into the fantasies he was recorded as uttering while out of his mind, including fears that sinful London was about to suffer a total deluge.

Their call for psychiatry to turn away from listening to the mentally ill did not stem from inhumanity, it was the logical consequence of their psychiatric credo, one that has been widely held. Mental illness, Hunter and Macalpine believed, was not psychogenic. Hence the utterances of the insane were but cries of distress—and not necessarily even good clues to its nature. You don't crack mental illness by decoding what the mad say: for, they held, mental disease had a biological base.

Powerful psychiatric currents have furthered such

tendencies to silence the insane, especially in institutional environments. From the Scientific Revolution, as we have already seen, influential views cast man essentially as a machine, and thus reduced the expressions and complaints of the disordered to secondary manifestations, the screeches and judderings of a faulty engine: something was wrong, but nothing significant was being said. In any case, did not the methods of the natural sciences prescribe observation and objectivity, not interaction and interpretation?

The noisiest patients were shunted off into the back wards, and all too often those who were shut up were, indeed, 'shut up'—or at least nobody attended to what they were uttering, there being less communication than excommunication. Visiting an Irish lunatic asylum around 1850, the inspectors were buttonholed by an inmate alleging theft: 'they took my language from me.' Similarly, the Romantic poet John Clare, locked up for several decades in various institutions, evolved a new language for his verse. Asked his reason, he responded:

'Why,' said he, 'they have cut off my head, and picked out all the letters of the alphabet—all the vowels and consonants—and brought them out through the ears; and then they want me to write poetry! I can't do it.'

Such protesters were not alone. John Perceval, author

of *A Narrative of the Treatment Received by a Gentleman, During a State of Mental Derangement* (1838), perhaps the most perceptive and poignant account ever written by an ex-patient about asylum life, voiced similar grievances. While a student at Oxford, Perceval, son of the assassinated Prime Minister Spencer Perceval, had undergone conversion to an extreme evangelical Protestant sect, which held that the Holy Ghost spoke pentecostally through believers, in a tongue resembling classical Greek. Soon he was being assailed by a pandemonium of voices, demonic no less than divine. Judged deranged by his family, he was confined to an asylum, which at least had the advantage that 'I might hollo or sing as my spirits commanded me'.

During his eighteen-month sojourn in two expensive and esteemed asylums, Perceval was to discover that (such was his experience) the medical staff never listened to his requests and barely addressed him as a human being—let alone as an English gentleman. He retaliated by holding his tongue. In the ensuing hostile silence,

> men acted as though my body, soul, and spirit were fairly given up to their control, to work their mischief and folly upon. My silence, I suppose, gave consent. I mean, that I was never told, such and such things we are going to do; we think it advisable to administer such

and such medicine, in this or that manner; I was never asked, Do you want any thing? do you wish for, prefer any thing? have you any objection to this or to that?

He was treated throughout, he accused, 'as if I were a piece of furniture, an image of wood, incapable of desire or will as well as judgement'. This refusal of the authorities to communicate with him proved, he was convinced, therapeutically counter-productive.

Similar experiences have been recorded by any number of ex-patients. In an exposé edited by two British Members of Parliament in 1957 and entitled *A Plea for the Silent*—perhaps *silenced* is better—one former inmate records the experience of ostracism in a mental institution:

> I was not allowed to write to my best friend to tell her where to locate me. . . . [T]he staff ignored me. . . .
> I thought that this technique must be a new method devised for the study of mental illness; but I was soon to learn that it appeared to be nothing but a callous belief that the insane do not suffer and that any problems they may express are bound to be 'imaginary'.

Numerous mad people's memoirs have claimed that there is (in Perceval's phrase) 'reasonableness in lunacy', that their thoughts are coherent and ought to be heeded. What trust, however, may be vested in the testimony of such crazy people? The manuscript autobiography, all half-million words of it, of the seventeenth-century Whig grandee, Goodwin Wharton, assures us that he impregnated his mistress, Mary Parish, 106 times, that he had liaisons with three queens of England, and that the Almighty personally instructed him to repopulate the kingdom.

And whom do we believe when we are faced with contested versions of reality? In his *The Interior of Bethlehem Hospital* (1818), Urbane Metcalf, a former inmate who claimed he was heir to the Danish throne, painted Bethlem as corrupt and brutalizing. For their part, the Hospital's records identify him as a trouble-maker. In such cases, historians must read between the lines and judge for themselves: contested readings of reality afford windows onto inter-subjectivities that never were univocal. Take Freud's Wolf Man, the Russian aristocrat Sergius P. He crops up three times, initially in Freud's 1920 analysis of his dream of white wolves with bushy tails, psychoanalytically decoded into a memory of the 'primal scene', his parents having sexual intercourse in his presence while he was a toddler. He next appears in a discussion of his subsequent analysis conducted by Ruth Mack Brunswick, herself analysed by Freud, in a volume with an introduction by Anna Freud (also analysed by her father), which claims the success of both Freudian analyses of Sergius. And finally, in the 1960s, he was interviewed by a journalist, Karin Obholzer. What, asked the reporter, did he make of Freud's reading of his dream? 'It's terribly far-fetched', responded Sergius. Wolf Man III has a very different tenor, but neither Freud's 'Wolf Man', nor Mack Brunswick's 'Wolf Man', nor the Wolf Man's 'Wolf Man' is to be taken at face value. Alerted thus to the dangers of monotonal readings, let us scrutinize the mind of an asylum patient, in part through his own words, as recorded by his physician.

Confused signals

James Tilley Matthews was a London tea merchant. Flushed, like Wordsworth, by the French Revolution's new dawn, he crossed to Paris in 1793. Deploring the outbreak of war between England and France, he got it into his head to mount a personal peace mission. Following an audience with Lord Liverpool, a senior minister in Pitt's administration, Matthews prepared to negotiate with the French authorities, but the Jacobin seizure of power wrecked his plans, and they had him clapped in jail.

Eventually released, he made his way back to England

in March 1796, convinced that he alone was privy to a dastardly French plot for 'surrendering to the French every secret of the British government, as for the republicanizing Great Britain and Ireland'. The secret weapon the French were mobilizing was Mesmerism, then all the rage in Paris. Teams of 'magnetic spies' had infiltrated England. Armed with 'air-looms', machines for transmitting waves of 'animal magnetism', they were stationing themselves in strategic sites 'near the Houses of Parliament, Admiralty, Treasury, etc.', where they would hypnotize members of the administration, so as to render them 'possessed', under a 'spell, like puppets'.

Being privy to all this, Matthews became Number One on the conspirators' hit list. A 'gang of seven', he alleged, had been sent to wipe him out, using their hypnotic 'science of assailment' to deploy tortures which included such atrocities as 'foot-curving, lethargy-making, spark-exploding, knee-nailing, burning out, eye-screwing, sight-stopping, roof-stringing, vital-tearing, fibre-ripping, etc.'. These threats to his life explained the urgency with which, on his return, Matthews sent warnings to Lord Liverpool, divulging the Jacobin plots. The minister must have been silent or sceptical, for Matthews tried a follow-up letter to him on 6 December 1796, which opened, 'I pronounce your Lordship to be in every sense of the word a most diabolical Traitor.'

Sensing Liverpool's 'treachery', Matthews proceeded to the House of Commons where he accused the Ministry of 'perfidious venality'. Examined before the Privy Council, he was committed in January 1797, his family's protests of his sanity being overridden by the Lord Chancellor.

Confined in Bethlem, Matthews felt utterly at the mercy of his persecutors. He turned to the universe for redress, penning a document beginning 'James, Absolute, Sole, Supreme, Sacred, Omni-Imperious, Arch-Grand, Arch-Sovereign . . . Arch Emperor', and offering rewards beyond the dreams of avarice to those who would assassinate his foes and secure his release, beginning at the bottom with 'three hundred thousand pounds sterling' for the head of the king of Norway and Denmark, and rising to a million pounds for the czar, a million for the emperor of China and the king of Spain, and so forth. Matthews gave directions as to method ('I shall prefer the Hanging them by the Neck till dead and afterwards Publickly burning them'), while apologizing for the barbarity of it all. It was, he explained, 'unfortunate for me . . . to have to put to death any one whomsoever'; yet necessity compelled him 'to punish rather than pity'.

But he remained inside. In 1809 his family pressed again for his release, and two distinguished physicians, Drs Birkbeck and Clutterbuck, testified to his sanity. They were opposed by the Bethlem medical staff, who argued that he was as obsessed as ever, 'sometimes an automaton moved by the agency of persons, or, at others, the Emperor of the whole world, hurling from their thrones the usurpers of his dominions'.

The best way to prove Matthews's continuing delusional state and the need for his detention, believed John Haslam, Bethlem's apothecary, was to let the patient speak for himself: and so he published Matthews's own story, taken from documents penned by his patient, in a mischievous volume entitled *Illustrations of Madness: Exhibiting a Singular Case of Insanity, And a No Less Remarkable Difference in Medical Opinions: Developing the Nature of an Assailment, And the Manner of Working Events; with a Description of the Tortures Experienced by Bomb-Bursting, Lobster-Cracking, and Lengthening the Brain. Embellished with a Curious Plate* (1810).

Here, as Haslam's title hinted, was yet another case in which not only the *mad* but the *mad-doctors* too could not see reason. 'Madness being the opposite of reason and good sense, as light is to darkness, straight to crooked, etc.', Haslam added with a palpable sneer, 'it appears wonderful that two opposite opinions could be entertained on the subject': were Clutterbuck and Birkbeck as mad as Matthews?

Matthews spent several more years in Bethlem—in fact, it was not he but Haslam who was 'released'. When Parliament enquired into the state of English mad-houses in 1815, Bethlem was discovered to be riddled with corruption—Haslam himself testified that its physician, John Monro, was an absentee and its recently deceased surgeon Bryan Crowther had for some years been so drunk and demented as to require a strait-jacket. Haslam was victimized, carpeted, and dismissed in 1816.

Perhaps this experience turned his mind, for later in life, the mad-doctor saw the whole of society as crazy. Testifying in court in an insanity plea, he contended that not only was the accused mad, but so too was everyone else—perhaps the only exception was Almighty God Himself (he had been reassured of God's soundness of mind, he respectfully added, on the authority of eminent Church of England divines). As mediated by Haslam, Matthews's story is thus one of mirrors and doubles: everyone is in his own turn deceiver and deceived, deranged and distrustful to the point of paranoia. Reason has become infinitely elusive.

Protest

Throughout the writings of the insane runs a wail of protest. Authors claim they were never crazy in the first place, or that they became mad only through the barbaric treatment meted out to them. As confinement increased, patients' protests grew with it. Cries went up from former inmates vindicating their sanity and alleging victimization by sinister foes, in publications ranging from the (already discussed) poetry of James Carkesse, to indictments by lesser-known figures.

Samuel Bruckshaw was a Stamford (Lincolnshire) merchant who in 1770 had a series of brushes with local officials. A conspiracy had been formed against him, he believed, to cheat him out of his property. His enemies, he records, then had him forcibly bundled off by two surgeons, who drove him to Ashton-under-Lyne in Lancashire, where he was confined in Wilson's private asylum and 'kept prisoner' for some nine months in an attic without a fire, abused by the attendants, poorly fed, and denied exercise. His letters were intercepted, though ultimately he secured release through the good offices of his brother. No pretence to treatment was offered.

Bruckshaw then vindicated himself in two pamphlets, *The Case, Petition and Address of Samuel Bruckshaw, who*

Suffered a Most Severe Imprisonment for Very Nearly a Whole Year (1774), and *One More Proof of the Iniquitous Abuse of Private Madhouses*, published in the same year. Interpreting them poses deep problems. Bruckshaw presents himself as a lamb led to the slaughter by diabolical conspiracies hatched by his fellow citizens. Yet his tone is, to say the least, fractious, suspicious, and litigious. And though he upholds his sanity, he records that while confined he had heard disembodied voices. In this and many similar cases, it would take a bold psycho-historian to judge whether such writings reveal persecution, paranoia, or both.

In *A Mind That Found Itself* (1908), Clifford Beers established himself as an all-American boy, of a 'truly American' family, descended from the earliest settlers. Born in New Haven in 1876, he went into business. Then calamity struck: he became 'neurasthenic', that distinctively American disease discussed in Chapter 6. Debilitated and distraught, in the summer of 1901 he made a half-hearted suicide attempt. Obviously, concluded his family, he needed treatment, and he was removed to Stamford Hall, a private 'sanatorium'. Until then, the young man had simply been neurasthenic; now he began to suffer hallucinations, believing he was the victim of an insidious conspiracy: those masquerading as his family were actually detectives in disguise.

As Beers later recalled, his paranoia was daily vindicated by his experiences. The callous treatment he received seemed like malicious torture, which would 'drive a sane man to violence'. 'My attendants', he wrote, much in the vein of Perceval, 'were incapable of understanding the operations of my mind, and what they could not understand they would seldom tolerate.' Everyone took his insanity as an invitation to brutality. In reality, Beers insisted, it would readily respond to reason.

It received none. Yet he recovered somewhat. In 1901, he spent some months with a private attendant, but was then placed in 1902 in the Hartford Retreat, another private but cheaper asylum which in its better days (see Chapter 5) had pioneered moral therapy. Beers continued to be driven by his delusions: he was under 'police surveillance' in an asylum full of 'detectives feigning insanity'; his food was poisoned, his 'friends' and 'family' just police stooges.

His sanity was restored not by the psychiatrists but by a fellow patient. Beers had become convinced that his 'brother' was a pretender. Put it to the test, a chum told him: write to your brother at his own address. Beers did. His brother arrived waving the letter. The scales fell from his eyes. 'Untruth became truth', unreason yielded to reason. He was born anew. 'My mind seemed

THE MAD

to have found itself.' He started redating time from his 'new birth'.

Depression turned to elation. Beers envisaged himself as a genius, an artist, or a pianist. And he made his views felt. There followed months of battles with the doctors. He grew demanding and, when his demands were not met, disruptive and destructive. This was, he records, not because he was intrinsically out of control, but because the asylum's cruelties provoked it. Placed under punitive discipline, he experienced the full horrors of the straitjacket. A sadistic assistant doctor (a 'Dr Jekyll and Mr Hyde') imposed forced feeding and medicines out of pure malice. Beers began recording every injustice—on scraps of paper, or sometimes by scribbling on the walls—as a record of crimes against humanity and as training for the great mission he was hatching, to become the 'saviour' of the insane.

When family funds again ran out, Beers was transferred to a state institution, the Connecticut Hospital for the Insane, where he was ignominiously classed as an 'indigent'. Once more the staff tyrannized him and he felt 'abandoned by everyone'. He fought back. 'I proceeded to assume entire charge of . . . the hospital'. Beers smuggled out letters to the state governor demanding investigations and campaigning for a bill of

26 A mentally ill patient in a straitjacket and strapped into a chair. Such chairs of restraint were meant to quieten maniacs by depriving them of the capacity to agitate themselves by violent motion; photograph after a wood-engraving, 1908.

rights for the insane, and developed utopian schemes for changing the world on his release.

Eventually, on 10 September 1903, his release was granted. Resuming work as a travelling salesman, in his spare time he composed his asylum autobiography, dictating 80,000 words in ninety hours. He astutely recognized that for his book to have maximum effect it was necessary to make friends not enemies. He started showing it to men of affairs and influence, to doctors and psychiatrists, gaining the support of such powerful medical establishment figures as William James and Weir Mitchell. When *A Mind That Found Itself* finally came out in 1908 it offered not just an indictment of the past, but a blueprint for the future: his dream baby, the Mental Hygiene Movement. From then on for the next twenty years, this archetypal salesman succeeded in selling to psychiatrists, policy-makers, and philanthropists his vision of a national crusade against mental illness, spearheaded by a new organization, the National Committee for Mental Hygiene. Its secretary, its leading spirit, its prize exhibit, was to be Beers himself. His is a moral tale of the tables turned, of patient turned healer.

Married to God

Beers's narrative is a cry of protest. Other writings by the 'mad' have been more by way of attempts to make strange experiences intelligible—to the world and probably also to themselves. The very first auto-biography in the English language is the work of an illiterate woman (she dictated it to a scribe) telling an uncomprehending public the truth of her religious transports.

Born around 1373, daughter to a prosperous King's Lynn burgess, Margery Kempe chronicled madness as a heaven-sent religious agony and ecstasy. Her initial bout of disturbance, after the birth of her first child, was a providential rap on the knuckles, delivered to rebuke a proud young lady, vulnerable to the Devil's tempta-tions. By His infinite mercy, the Almighty had returned her to her 'right mind', and rescued her from sin. Still she remained wedded to this world, and it took the failure of the brewery she owned—her ale went providentially flat—to humble and turn her from wickedness.

Having suffered childbed insanity and business col-lapse, Margery Kempe experienced an overwhelming call to cut herself off from the world, convinced that, by contrast to conditions on earth, it was 'merry in heaven'. Her attempts to follow divine signposts met enduring hostility. 'Woman, give up this life that you lead, and go and spin, and card wool, as other women do,' she was told by the worldlings.

Sickened by the flesh, Margery sought release from human bondage. She fasted, did penance, and clad herself in a hair shirt. Above all, she strove to free herself from sexual slavery, knowing (following St Augustine's reflections) how offensive to God was the pleasure she and her husband had taken in carnal delights. She told him she now loved God alone and begged him to accept a chastity pact. Eventually he signed away his conjugal rights in return for her paying his debts.

Despite this apprentice mortification, she remained vainglorious: 'she thought that she loved God more than He loved her,' she was to recall. In that state, she was prey to the Devil's snares. He set a trap of lechery. A man made a pass at her. Flattered, she surrendered, only at the last moment to be spurned. Mortified, she craved Christ's forgiveness; it was granted, and, in return, her Saviour promised her a lifelong hairshirt in her heart. Thereafter, tribulations were secret signs of holiness.

She began seeing visions, and these were accompanied by the copious bouts of weeping which attended her to the end of her days. She would also informally shrive penitents (something normally reserved for priests). A 'miracle' secured her escape when a piece of masonry falling from a church struck but did not harm her.

Margery's religious observances brought public reproof. Her weeping bouts were detested, she was called 'false hypocrite', and her friends were advised to abandon her. Furthermore, she was accused of having the Devil in her and of being a 'false Lollard'—that is, heretic. But such trials enhanced her awareness of the divine indwelling. When she heard mention of Christ's Passion, she would swoon in ecstasy and experience divine music. The Lord called her His mother, sister, and daughter.

Initially Margery was perturbed. Might these voices and visions be the temptations of the Devil? Seeking guidance, she consulted the mystic Dame Julian of Norwich, from whom she received reassurance: those were not imaginings of her own devising but truly manifestations from God. Margery grew more confident of her religious calling, winning a reputation as a woman with a divine vocation. She acquired minor prophetic powers. One day, she predicted a terrible storm: it came about.

Eventually, she set off on pilgrimage to the Holy Land. Proximity to the scenes of Christ's Passion led her to weep and wail more than ever and to 'wrestle with her body'. Some thought she was puffed up with 'pretence and hypocrisy', or, suffering from epilepsy. Others accused her of drunkenness. Still others believed she had been possessed by an evil spirit. Her fellow English pilgrims found her a nuisance, with her continual wailing and the ceaseless rebukes she directed towards them, and sometimes they forced her to leave their party. Similar tribulations also beset her in England. 'Evil talk' about her grew, and many said she had the Devil in her. She ran the risk of imprisonment, for the authorities looked with suspicion upon this wife and mother gallivanting around the country in the guise of a holy woman, berating the ungodly and urging wives to leave their husbands and follow God.

All the while, her love of God grew. She overheard conversations about her between God the Father and Jesus. Her attention became fixed upon the 'manhood' of Christ, but it was the Godhead Himself who finally married her. 'I must be intimate with you and lie in your bed with you,' the Father told her, 'take me to you as your wedded husband. ... Kiss my mouth, my head, and my feet as sweetly as you want.' The earlier sexual temptations which she had undergone were not, however, entirely a thing of the past, and in time she was visited by 'abominable visions', conjured up by the

Devil, of threatening male genitals to which she was commanded to prostitute herself. Temporarily she felt forsaken, but she recovered. At another point, she was overcome by a desire to kiss male lepers; stick to women, her confessor advised.

Should we see Margery as turned by puerperal insanity, or think of her as a mystic? Despite modern attempts to pin contemporary psychiatric labels on her, there is no master key to Margery's mind, and no one right way of reading her life. She knew that many thought her voices and visions signified madness, attributed to disease or the Devil: she pondered deeply, and sought advice. But the path to which she aspired—a spiritual communion, marriage even, with God—was legitimate within the beliefs of her times, though one, of course, exceptionally liable to misunderstanding.

Making madness visible

The disturbed have expressed themselves not just *verbally*, in countless autobiographical outpourings, but *visually* too, by drawing, painting, and making things. Long before 'art therapy' was recognized, it was not unknown for asylum patients to be permitted to draw on humanitarian grounds: James Tilley Matthews, just discussed, himself depicted the infernal machines assailing his consciousness—he also submitted high-quality architectural designs for a new building for Bethlem. And his contemporary, Jonathan Martin, who had partly succeeded in burning down York Minster in protest against the ungodliness of his times, drew himself, while under confinement, as the instrument of God's wrath and of divine vengeance, descending upon London, the modern Babylon. (His brother, John, was a successful artist.) The artist Richard Dadd, probably a victim of sunstroke while travelling in the Near East, murdered his father and was confined to Bethlem, and there and in Broadmoor, under official encouragement, he painted for the rest of his life, undertaking his most acclaimed canvases, including *Contradiction: Oberon and Titania* and *The Fairy Feller's Fatal Stoke.*

It was not until the 1870s that psychiatric attention was paid to the image-making of the mad, in the belief that it might be diagnostically revelatory. One pioneer was Cesare Lombroso, who outlined a pathography of the insane imagination in accordance with his theories of atavistic degenerationism. Some of the vast assemblage of the art of the insane which he collected was reproduced in his *The Man of Genius.* By juxtaposing it with the work of children, 'defectives', and people from 'primitive cultures', he 'discovered' what he identified as certain perennial traits symptomatic of the crazed, infantile, or savage psyche. The paintings of the insane, according to Lombroso, were characterized by distortion, originality, imitation, repetition, absurdity, arabesques, eccentricity, obscenity, and, above all, symbolism—a rather comprehensively incriminatory list.

The implied moral was that if the mad painted like that, then those who painted like that were mad. And that was precisely the verdict passed by certain psychiatrists upon Expressionists, Surrealists, and other avant-garde artists. Cézanne and the Cubists were suffering from neurological eye complaints, judged Theodore Hyslop, physician to Bethlem, no mean artist himself and author of *The Great Abnormals* (1925).

Psychiatrists might be excused for drawing such connections. After all, as heirs to the 'mad genius' tradition discussed in Chapter 4, artists like Ernst Kirschner, Max Ernst, Paul Klee, and Antonin Artaud publicly flouted civilized restraint and gloried in the irrational, singling out lunatics, children, and primitives as those truly in touch with the wellsprings of feeling, unlike sterile academic artists and bourgeois critics. And they tried to emulate those they envied: Oskar Kokoschka painted himself as a degenerate, long before the organizers of Hitler's notorious exhibition of 'Entartete

27 Cesare Lombroso (1836–1909) was an Italian criminologist with psychiatric and anthropological interests. He endorsed degenerationist theories, and undertook psychiatric studies of criminality and genius, and the art of the insane; photogravure, *c.*1900.

Kunst' (degenerate art), held in Munich in 1937, diagnosed and denounced modern art en masse as psychopathological.

Meanwhile, asylum superintendents and psychiatrists began to encourage patients to paint, less in expectation of finding Lombrosian evidence of pathography, than psychotherapeutically, in hopes that their creative artistic processes would shed light on the deep and dark recesses of the mind. In a private asylum near Bern, Dr Walter Morgenthaler encouraged the extraordinary patient-painter Adolf Wölfli, while the scholar Hans Prinzhorn and the painter Jean Dubuffet were active in establishing collections of the art of the insane, not as diagnostic but as rewarding in its own right.

Art as psychotherapy also became popular, though the danger lurked that—rather as with Charcot's hand-picked hysterics—patients would end up being unconsciously coached to produce artworks according to psychiatric expectations. The decline of the asylum and today's turn to drug therapies may toll the knell of the genre.

Maybe that would be no bad thing. Artistic and psychiatric conventions over the centuries stereotyped the mad, thereby perpetuating scapegoating prejudices. It is questionable whether the identification of a distinct genre served any useful diagnostic or therapeutic purpose. When Van Gogh painted himself, who can say whether he was painting madness?—all that is clear is that he was painting misery.

The century of psychoanalysis?

Science and psychiatry

Psychiatry has typically pursued twin goals: gaining a scientific grasp of mental illness, and healing the mentally ill. These have generally been seen as inseparable, but at times one has been emphasized more than another. In the late nineteenth century the priority lay, for many psychiatrists, upon establishing their discipline as a truly scientific enterprise, capable of taking its rightful place in the pantheon of the 'hard' biomedical sciences, alongside neurology and pathology, and utterly distinct from such quackish and fringy embarrassments as mesmerism and spiritualism. Providing psychiatry with a sound scientific basis was particularly important at that time, on account of its strong positivistic and Darwinian leanings. The great student of epilepsy, John Hughlings Jackson, for instance, drew on Herbert Spencer to make evolutionism the basis for his accounts of nervous dysfunction, while Henry Maudsley developed a psychiatric outlook grounded in Darwinian biology. Freud for his part was also a passionate admirer of Darwin and famously wanted to achieve a 'Copernican' revolution in his field. For the leading German Emil Kraepelin (1856–1926), it was essential to shed the unscientific dross which had gathered around psychiatry.

Following an early appointment at Dorpat University (in Estonia, then in Prussia), Kraepelin became professor at the university clinic at Heidelberg, a principal centre of German medicine. His career marks the culmination of a century of descriptive clinical psychiatry and psychiatric nosology. Downplaying the sufferer's psychopathological state in favour of the 'disease entity', he approached his patients as symptom-carriers, and his case histories concentrated on the core signs of each disorder. The course of psychiatric illness, he insisted, offered the best clue to its nature, rather than, as in common practice, the raft of symptoms the patient showed at a particular moment.

On this basis, Kraepelin wrought a great innovation in disease concepts and classification. Amalgamating Morel's *démence précoce* with the notion of *hebephrenia* (psychosis in the young, marked by regressive behaviour) developed by Karl Kahlbaum and his pupil

Ewald Hecker, he launched the model of a degenerative condition which he named *dementia praecox*, to be decisively distinguished from manic-depressive psychoses (Falret's 'circular insanity'). The archetypal *dementia praecox* sufferer as pictured by Kraepelin on the basis of meticulous clinical experience might be astute and clever, but he seemed to have forsaken his humanity, abandoned all desire to participate in society, and withdrawn into a solipsistic world of his own, perhaps mute, violent, and paranoid. Kraepelin routinely used phrases like 'atrophy of the emotions' and 'vitiation of the will' to convey the sense that they were moral perverts, psychopaths, almost a species apart. As the precursor to schizophrenia, Kraepelin's *dementia praecox* has left an indelible mark on modern psychiatry.

Kraepelin's commitment to the natural history of mental disorders led him to track the entire life histories of his patients in a longitudinal perspective which privileged prognosis (likely outcome) as definitive of the disorder. An admirer of the experimental psychologist Wilhelm Wundt, he also pioneered psychological testing for psychiatric patients. Among Kraepelin's colleagues was Alois Alzheimer (1864–1915), whose research into senile dementia led to the major specialty of psycho-geriatrics. Driven thus by a stern research ethos, his Munich clinic inspired similar establishments elsewhere, including the hospital which Henry Maudsley set up, by bequest, in South London, designed (uniquely in England) to be not an asylum but rather a research centre.

While heredity played a certain part in his conceptual apparatus, Kraepelin was critical of French degenerationist theory—a point he shared with Freud, though the two generally had little in common. Holding out slight expectations of successful treatment, Kraepelin, like the degenerationists, was gloomy about the outcome of major psychiatric disorders, especially *dementia praecox*. By 1900 Pinelian optimism had thus run into the sands: 'we know a lot and can do little,' commented one German asylum doctor. To many the psychiatrist seemed to have been reduced to acting as society's policeman or gatekeeper, protecting it from the insane. Endorsed by eugenism and degenerationism, a psychiatric politics was emerging in which it could soon be decided that the very lives of the mentally ill were not 'worth living'; in the 1930s, Nazi psychiatry deemed schizophrenics, no less than Jews, ripe for elimination. Between January 1940 and September 1942, in what might be seen as a trial run for the 'final solution', 70,723 mental patients were gassed, chosen from lists of those whose 'lives were not worth living' drawn up by nine leading professors of psychiatry and thirty-nine top physicians.

Psychodynamics

Partly in reaction against the pessimism of asylum psychiatry and the dogmatism of the somatists, new styles of dynamic psychiatry were launched and won support. Their historical roots include Franz Anton Mesmer's therapeutic explorations, in Enlightenment Vienna and Paris, of 'animal magnetism'. Bringing to light as it did multiple dissociations of personality and automatism of behaviour, such psychiatric recourse to hypnotism unearthed hitherto hidden strata of the self and raised issues about the will, the unconscious, and the unity of the person. All notion of a Cartesian cogito was now shattered; even before Freud, it was becoming clear that man was not master in his own house.

Drawing upon mesmeric techniques, the mysteries of the psyche were investigated in Nancy by A. A. Liébault and H. M. Bernheim, while in Paris the great Charcot made hypnotism a diagnostic device for exposing hysteria: only hysterics could be hypnotized, he believed (the Nancy school demurred). What he failed to notice —his critics were not so gullible—was that the hysterical behaviour of his 'star' hysterics, young working-class women, far from being objective phenomena ripe for scientific investigation, were artefacts produced within the supercharged theatrical atmosphere of the Salpêtrière. Charcot deceived himself into thinking his patients' behaviours were natural rather than 'performances', the products of suggestion. The months Freud spent studying under Charcot in Paris in 1885 proved crucial to his development—which is one reason why psychoanalysis has never been able to shake off the charge that its 'cures', no less than Charcot's, are largely products of suggestion.

The conquistador of the unconscious

Born to a middle-class Jewish family initially from Moravia (modern Czech Republic) and trained in Vienna in medicine and physiology, Sigmund Freud (1856-1939) initially specialized in clinical neurology. An enthusiastic Darwinist and a protégé of the hard-nosed neurophysiologist Ernst Brücke, he brought a materialist approach to the study of mankind, deeming mind reducible to brain and all his life disparaging religion as 'an illusion'. Working with Josef Breuer (1842–1925), he became alerted to the affinities between hypnotic states, hysteria, and the neuroses. Breuer told him about one of his patients, 'Anna O.', whose bizarre hysterical symptoms he had been treating by inducing hypnotic states and systematically leading her back, under hypnosis, to the onset of each symptom. On re-experiencing the precipitating traumas, the hysterical symptom in question vanished, so Breuer claimed.

The time he spent under Charcot in Paris gave Freud theoretical insights into Breuer's experiences—not least a hint of the sexual origin of hysteria: 'c'est toujours la chose génitale', Charcot had whispered to him, privately (the public Charcot kept sex out of his explanations). Freud and Breuer began a close collaboration which resulted in 1895 in the publication of their *Studies on Hysteria*, but by then Freud was already going beyond his senior colleague and working on the idea that neurosis stemmed from early *sexual* traumas. His hysterical female patients, he concluded, had been subjected to pre-pubescent 'seduction'—that is, in most cases, sexual abuse by the father; repressed memories of such assaults later surfaced, he concluded, in otherwise baffling hysterical symptoms. This 'seduction theory' was spelt out to his Berlin friend Wilhelm Fliess in May 1893, and during the next three years Freud's enthusiasm for his shocking hypothesis grew until, on 21 April 1896, he finally went public with it in a lecture in Vienna on the aetiology of hysteria.

The next year, however, on 21 September 1897, he confessed to Fliess: 'I no longer believe in my *neurotica*'—that is, the seduction theory. By then Freud, deep in richly autobiographical dreams and self-analysis, had convinced himself that his patients' seduction stories were fantasies, originating not in the perverse deeds of adults but in the erotic wishes of infants. The collapse of the seduction theory ushered in the idea of infantile sexuality within the Oedipus complex, first disclosed to Fliess a month later:

> I have found love of the mother and jealousy of the father in my own case too, and now believe it to be a general phenomenon of early childhood . . . if that is the case, the gripping power of *Oedipus Rex*, in spite of all the rational objections to the inexorable fate that the story presupposes, becomes intelligible . . . Every member of the audience was once a budding Oedipus in phantasy . . .

Throughout his career, Freud stood by the cardinal importance of this breakthrough: 'if psychoanalysis could boast of no other achievement than the discovery of the repressed Oedipus complex, that alone would give a claim to be included among the precious new acquisitions of mankind.' The twin pillars of psychoanalysis—the workings of the unconscious and Oedipal sexuality—thus emerged from Freud's volte-face: without the abandonment of the seduction theory, psychoanalysis as a theoretical edifice built upon unconscious libidinal desires and their repression could not exist.

How to explain this decisive switch remains hotly contested. Orthodox Freudians, notably Freud's disciple and biographer Ernest Jones, have cast it as the 'Eureka-moment' in which he saw the light. Some critics allege, by contrast, a loss of nerve, and hold that it was the abandonment of the seduction theory that was the error, perhaps even a 'betrayal' both of psycho-sexual truth and of his patients. (If they had indeed been sexually abused, their stories were now dis-counted, as were those of future generations of patients on the couch.) This 'betrayal' has been associated with the cool reception of Freud's Vienna lecture, and with the death of his father in October 1896. Thenceforth Papa Sigmund stood in father Jacob's shoes, and psychoanalysis thus became a screen for the sins of the father. The most likely explanation is that Freud had become preoccupied with the role of fantasy in people's lives, and especially in their neuroses.

Freud grew distanced from Breuer, who favoured the

use of hypnotic techniques, which Freud never mastered, and he also broke with Fliess, whose approach was more biological. In a string of profoundly original works beginning with his *magnum opus, The Interpretation of Dreams* (1900), Freud advanced the fundamental theoretical postulates of psychoanalysis: unconscious mental states, their repression, and the ensuing neurotic consequences; infantile sexuality, and the symbolic meaning of dreams and hysterical symptoms. He also outlined the investigative techniques of free association and dream interpretation—two methods for overcoming resistance and uncovering hidden unconscious wishes—and he elucidated what clinical practice had revealed to him: therapeutic transference. Much of this was summed up in his *Introductory Lectures* (1916–17).

During the Great War Freud applied his ideas about the psychogenesis of hysterical symptoms to shellshock and other war neuroses: soldiers displaying paralysis and loss of sight, speech, and hearing with no palpable organic basis were said to be suffering from conversion hysteria. Though he was still in principle committed to the scientific biology in which he had been trained, in actuality Freud's psychodynamics proceeded without reference to neurological substrates.

In his later years, while continuing to elaborate his individual psychology—notably the notion of developmental phases, the conflict between eros and the death instinct (thanatos), and the ego, superego, and id—Freud extended his speculations into the social, historical, cultural, and anthropological spheres, producing theories about the origins of the incest taboo, about patriarchy and monotheism, and about the neurotic springs of the religious and artistic impulses. His endlessly fertile, if obsessive, mind also shed light on many other mental manifestations, like jokes and 'Freudian slips'.

Freud's ideas proved crucial for favoured twentieth-century views of the self, amongst them belief in the dynamic unconscious and the insights into it afforded by free association; the meaning of dreams; repression and defence mechanisms; infantile sexuality; the sexual foundations of neurosis and the therapeutic potential of transference. Though he liked to see himself as a natural scientist, his beliefs were fated to enjoy their greatest acclaim and influence in fiction, art, and films. With his disturbing view of a self which was divided and not master in its own house, Freud became the principal myth-maestro of the twentieth century.

The psychoanalytical movement

In creative tension with Vienna, a vigorous tradition of depth psychiatry emerged in Switzerland. At Burghölzli, the Zürich psychiatric hospital, Eugen Bleuler (1857–1939) deployed psychoanalytic theories in his delineations of 'schizophrenia', his term for the condition he honed from Kraepelin's *dementia praecox*, one marked by delusions, hallucinations, and disordered thought. Such schizophrenics were 'strange, puzzling, inconceivable, uncanny, incapable of empathy, sinister, frightening'. But it was Carl Jung's (1875–1961) influence which prevailed, especially after his break with Freud in 1912, when he developed his alternative 'analytical psychology'—a less sexual and more idealistic rendering of the unconscious.

A pastor's son, Jung trained in medicine in his native Basel before specializing in psychiatry. After meeting Freud in 1907, he became the master's favourite son, gaining a reputation as the 'crown prince' of psychoanalysis—or its non-Jewish frontman. Oedipal conflicts flared, however, exacerbated in 1912 when his *The Psychology of the Unconscious* challenged many of Freud's key theories, notably the sexual origin of the neuroses; within two years the rift was total and final—the first of the epic feuds which balkanized psychoanalysis and undermined its scientific pretensions.

The analytic psychology developed by Jung claimed to offer a more rounded view than Freud's of the psyche and its various personality types, including the 'extra-vert' and 'introvert' announced in his *Psychological Types* (1921). A healthy balance of opposites was to be prized (animus and anima, the male and female sides of the personality), as was the integration of thought, feeling, and intuition. Jung proposed the existence of a 'collect-ive unconscious', stocked with latent memories from mankind's ancestral past, passed down from generation to generation by some Lamarckian inheritance of acquired characteristics mechanism. Studies of dreams, of art and anthropology fed a fascination with arche-types and myths (e.g. the earth mother), which were said to fill that collective unconscious, shaping experi-ence and, as stressed in his final book, *Man and His Symbols* (1964), constituting the springs of creativity. With its vision of the self realized in the integrated personality, Jung's analytic psychiatry retains its inspirational appeal as a personal philosophy of life.

France developed psychodynamic traditions of its own which left it relatively impervious to Freud—at least prior to the pyrotechnic prominence enjoyed in the 1970s by the maverick Jacques Lacan, who read

Freud through a structuralist semiotics. In the wake of Charcot, Pierre Janet (1859–1947) elaborated theories of personality development and mental disorders which long dominated French dynamic psychiatry. Exploring the unconscious, he left sensitive clinical descriptions of hysteria, anorexia, amnesia, and obsessional neuroses—and of their treatment with hypnosis, suggestion, and other psycho-dynamic techniques. Correlating hysteria with what he called 'subconscious fixed ideas', he proposed treating it with 'psychological analysis'.

Though Freud took a dim view of American society, psychoanalysis found a particularly receptive environment in the New World. Many key analysts migrated there, even before the Nazi persecution of Jews. Amongst the earliest was Alfred Adler (1870–1937), best remembered for his notion of the inferiority complex: the neurotic individual overcompensating by manifesting aggression. After participating in Freud's psychoanalytic circle in its early years, Adler broke with the master and elaborated his own theory in *The Nervous Character* (1912). Moving to the USA, he turned his attention to the relations between individual and environment, stressing the need for social harmony as the means to avoid neurosis. His views became central to the commitment of interwar American psychiatry to a vision of social integration and stability based on individual 'adjustment' and adaptation to healthy social forms.

With so many Jewish practitioners forced to flee Europe, the United States became the world head-quarters of psychoanalysis, and by the mid-twentieth century American psychiatry at large, in university departments and teaching hospitals, was heavily psycho-analytically oriented. Writing in the 1960s, two psycho-analytically oriented American practitioners, Franz G. Alexander and Sheldon T. Selesnick, could pro-nounce, with assurance, that 'psychiatry has come of age'.

Psychoanalysis spread far more slowly and partially to the United Kingdom, by contrast, due perhaps to Anglo-Saxon phlegm and distrust of navel-gazing. An early supporter, David Eder, recalled addressing a paper in 1911 to the Neurological Section of the British Medical Association on a case of hysteria treated by Freudian methods: at the end of his talk, the entire audience, including the Chairman, walked out in stony silence. Small wonder, with psychiatrists around like the venerable Charles Mercier, who gloated in 1916

> that psychoanalysis is past its perihelion, and is rapidly retreating into the dark and silent depths from which it emerged. It is well that it should be systematically described before it goes to join pounded toads and sour milk in the limbo of discarded remedies.

Despite such 'resistance', inroads were nevertheless made, sped perhaps by the crisis in standard explanations produced by shell shock in the Great War. The thought of mass cowardice was too dreadful to contemplate but no regular psychiatry could explain why brave men of good background all of a sudden could no longer fight.

Early British psychoanalysis crystallized around Ernest Jones (1879–1958). A founder of the London Society of Psychoanalysis (1913), this Welshman, whose zest, vanity, and phenomenal energies made him a born proselytizer, became a close friend of Freud and eventually his biographer, and in 1912 he brought out the first book published in England in this field: *Papers on Psycho-Analysis*. Later, the London scene was animated by the theoretical battles waged by Melanie Klein (1882–1960) and Anna Freud (1895–1982), who had fled to England with her father in 1938 after the Nazi occupation of Austria: Freudians and Kleinians unforgettably crossed swords over the interpretation of infant/mother relations. In London the Tavistock Clinic, founded in 1920, promoted psychotherapy, especially for children and families, and fostered the British 'object relations' school. From the 1940s, great faith was vested by Donald Winnicott and John Bowlby in the nuclear family, and particularly the mother, as the sheet anchor of psychosocial adjustment.

In time, the infiltration of broadly psychodynamic turns of thinking helped the idea to gain ground—it had become conventional by the 1950s—that mental disorder was not confined to the certifiable. Ordinary people might have 'complexes', and neuroses, it was now said, ran like a watermark through the population at large: housewife blues, family conflicts, alcoholism, adolescent adjustment problems, generational tensions, and so much more—the precursors of the depression, eating, and sexual disorders ubiquitous by the close of the century.

By the 1950s, pop culture had created new and even glamorous psychological types like the juvenile delinquent—the slumming modern version of the melancholy poet or Romantic genius. The 'psychiatrization of everything' predictably occurred first in the United States—a trend deliciously mocked in Leonard Bernstein's musical, *West Side Story* (1956), in which the crazy-mixed-up young New Yorkers taunt a police officer on the warpath:

> Officer Krupke, you're really a square;
> This boy don't need a judge, he needs an analyst's care!
> It's just his neurosis that oughta be curbed,
> He's psychologic'ly disturbed.

The shock of the new

While Freud was being lionized by the avant-garde as the conquistador of the unconscious, the medical treatment of the institutionalized saw striking therapeutic innovations, some effective, many dubious, a few dangerous. In the wake of the new microbiology, the effects of bacterial infections on brain pathology were identified, beginning with syphilis; and in Vienna Julius von Wagner-Jauregg (1857–1940) found that counter-infection with artificially induced malaria was effective against general paresis of the insane. This discovery—an effective treatment against a familiar and terrible condition—won him the Nobel Prize in 1927: he remains the only psychiatrist so honoured.

Wagner-Jauregg himself was one of many advocates of Faradization (electric-shock) treatment for that new disorder, shell shock. Prolonged-sleep therapies, induced by barbiturates, then enjoyed a hazardous vogue in the 1920s. Pioneered by Manfred Sakel, insulin-induced coma—insulin had been introduced against diabetes in 1922—was employed from the 1930s against schizophrenia and, though dangerous, it apparently brought some benefit. Shock treatments of many kinds thus came into vogue.

Working with epileptics, the Budapest psychiatrist

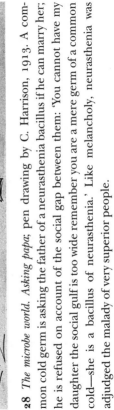

28 *The microbe world. Asking papa;* pen drawing by C. Harrison, 1913. A common cold germ is asking the father of a neurasthenia bacillus if he can marry her; he is refused on account of the social gap between them: 'You cannot have my daughter the social gulf is too wide remember you are a mere germ of a common cold—she is a bacillus of neurasthenia.' Like melancholy, neurasthenia was adjudged the malady of very superior people.

Ladislaus Joseph von Meduna developed a different shock treatment in which a camphor-like drug (marketed as Cardiazol, Metrazol in the USA) was the convulsive agent, producing seizures so violent that patients sometimes suffered broken bones. The theory underpinning Meduna's innovation was that epileptiform seizures naturally produced improvements in schizophrenics so why not induce them artificially? And then in 1938, at his neuropsychiatric clinic in Genoa, Ugo Cerletti (1877–1963) began to use electric shocks (ECT) to alleviate severe depression—a treatment with a highly controversial history—it became a key target for psychiatry's critics—though some measure of success.

Psychosurgery too enjoyed a vogue from the 1930s. At Lisbon University, the neurologist Egas Moniz (1874–1955) claimed that obsessive and depressive cases could be improved by leucotomy, surgical severance of the connections between the frontal lobes and the rest of the brain. Lobotomy and leucotomy were enthusiastically taken up in the United States, spearheaded by Dr Walter Freeman, a neurologist at George Washington University Hospital (Washington, DC). Often using an ordinary cocktail-cabinet ice-pick, inserted, via the eye-socket, with a few taps from a carpenter's hammer, Freeman at one point was getting through a hundred transorbital lobotomies a week—he performed some 3,600 in all. By 1951 over 18,000 patients in the USA had undergone lobotomy, before it was overtaken by growing doubts, and by the psychopharmacological revolution.

Psychosurgery was a plausible try—was it not likely that behaviour modification could be achieved through direct surgical intervention into the brain? The neurophysiological advances discussed in Chapter 6 had shown that specific cortical centres controlled particular aspects of cognition and affect, and though the front brain remained somewhat of a mystery, animal experiments suggested that it might be implicated in mental balance. Furthermore, surgery had established itself as the cutting-edge of medicine. From the humble tonsillectomy upwards, operations had become routine, increasingly safe, and even fashionable. Surgeons, stated the *New York Times* in 1936, 'now think no more of operations on the brain than they do of removing an appendix'. Like other shock treatments, lobotomy held out promise not just for the mentally ill but for psychiatry itself. That speciality had been bumping along the bottom in the early decades of the century, bemired by the unsavoury associations of huge, squalid public warehouses for the mad poor. Psychosurgery promised to change all that—to turn no-hope asylums into true hospitals, rescue psychiatry through the knife, and thus provide a lifeline for the discipline back into mainstream general medicine. In any case, what else was to be done with the half-a-million lost souls in America's asylums living in the concentration-camp conditions soon to be exposed by Albert Deutsch's chilling *The Shame of the States* (1948)? Any attempt at cure seemed better than none—did not the old medical adage state that desperate conditions required desperate remedies?

And psychosurgery seemed to work. Rescued from crippling agitational states, some lobotomized patients were discharged from institutions and went on to hold down jobs and family roles—becoming, in the classic Adlerian sense, well adjusted. Lobotomy was claimed to be particularly effective at turning the troublesome into 'quiet, placid, uncomplaining persons who showed little concern about their troubles'—submissive souls who, even if they never achieved institutional discharge, would nevertheless thereafter be model patients.

Psychosurgery and other shock therapies signal the wish of well-meaning psychiatrists to do something for psychiatry's forgotten patients; they have, in turn, been criticized for being grotesque, quackish, brutal, and hubristic. Invasive treatments equally reflect the powerlessness of patients in the face of arrogant and reckless doctors, and the ease with which they became experimental fodder. In a now notorious experiment, hundreds of black mental patients at the Tuskeegee Asylum in Alabama were guinea pigs without their knowledge or consent in an experiment to test long-term responses to syphilis, a minor echo of the atrocities committed by Nazi psychiatrists.

The chemical revolution

Penicillin was introduced in the 1940s, and in the wake of the antibiotics miracle, great expectations rose for psychopharmacology. Replacing the old standby blank cartridges like bromides and croton oil, and also the dangerous amphetamines widely used in the 1930s, lithium, the first psychotropic (mood-influencing) drug, was introduced in 1949 to manage manic-depression. Anti-psychotic and anti-depressant compounds, notably the phenothiazines (chlorpromazine, marketed as 'Largactil'—called by critics the 'liquid cosh') and Imipramine (for depression) were developed by the research laboratories of drugs companies in the early 1950s. They made it possible for many patients to leave or avoid the sheltered but numbing environment of the psychiatric hospital, and maintain life, under continuing medication, in the outside world. The top British psychiatrist William Sargant heralded the new drugs as a blessed deliverance from the shadowland of the asylum and the follies of Freud— they enabled doctors to 'cut the cackle', he crowed, boldly predicting that the new psychotropics would eliminate mental illness by the year 2000. Psycho-pharmacology certainly brought a therapeutic boost to the psychiatric profession, promising as it did a cost-effective method of alleviating suffering without recourse to lengthy hospital stays, psychoanalysis, or irreversible surgery. It would also promote psychiatry's wishful identity as a branch of general medicine.

The new drugs enjoyed phenomenal success. The tranquillizer Valium (diazepam) became the world's most widely prescribed medication in the 1960s; by 1970 one American woman in five was using minor tranquillizers; and by 1980 American physicians were writing ten million prescriptions a year for anti-depressants alone, mostly 'tricyclics' like Imipramine. Introduced in 1987, Prozac, which raises serotonin levels and so enhances a 'feelgood' sense of security and assertiveness, was being prescribed almost ad lib for depression; within five years, eight million people had taken that 'designer' anti-depressant, said to make people feel 'better than well'. Central nervous system drugs are currently the leading class of medicines sold in the USA, accounting for a quarter of all sales. With the immense success of the anti-psychotic, anti-manic, and anti-depressant drugs introduced in the last half of the twentieth century, organic psychiatry is arguably in danger of becoming drug-driven, a case of the tail wagging the dog.

By permitting treatment of the mentally disturbed on an outpatient basis, psycho-active drugs have substantially reduced the numbers of those institutionalized. But problems of side-effects and dependency are perennial, and their long-term effects are necessarily unknown. Major ethical and political questions hang over recourse to pharmaceutical products to reshape personalities, especially when the development, manufacture, and marketing of such drugs lie in the hands of monopolistic multinationals.

Anti-psychiatry and the asylum

Psychotropic drugs seemed to offer hopes of delivery from the asylum problem as psychiatrists in Europe and America grew increasingly critical of the old mental hospitals pitting the landscape. Deficiencies in the day-to-day management of English asylums had long been exposed, ever since the damning indictment of neglect and casual cruelty contained in Montagu Lomax's *The Experiences of an Asylum Doctor, with Suggestions for Asylum and Lunacy Law Reform* (1921), a sobering work written not by a protesting patient but by a disillusioned doctor. 'Our asylums detain', he complained, 'but they certainly do not cure.'

Not least, the rigid segregation of the sane from the mad which the asylum had implemented no longer seemed to make epidemiological sense. Modern psychiatry came to the conclusion that the greatest proportion of mental disorders was in reality to be found not in the asylum but in the community at large—emphasis was newly falling upon neuroses not severe enough to warrant certification and long-term hospitalization. 'Gone forever', insisted the American psychiatrist Karl Menninger in 1956, 'is the notion that the mentally ill person is an exception. It is now accepted that most people have some degree of mental illness at some time'—cynics might say that psychiatry was thus making a pitch for the entire population.

Attention shifted to 'milder' and 'borderline' cases, and mental abnormality began to be seen as part of normal variability. A new social psychiatry was formulated, whose remit extended over the populace at large. This dissolving of the divide between sane and insane had momentous practical consequences for custody and care. As attention shifted from institutional provision per se to the clinical needs of the patient, policy pointed in the direction of the 'unlocked door' prompting experiments with outpatients' clinics and psychiatric day hospitals, and encouraging treatments with an eye to discharge. Such developments presaged the end of custodial management as the routine course of action.

The transition took many forms, presided over by many philosophies of change. Some hoped to effect a modernization of the mental hospital from within. From the late 1940s a few English mental hospitals unlocked their doors, and 'therapeutic communities' were also set up, units of up to a hundred, in which physicians and patients were to cooperate in the creation of more positive therapeutic environments, which would erode the old authoritarian hierarchies dividing staff and inmates and encourage shared decision-making in a more relaxed atmosphere.

Others demanded something far more drastic, notably the champions of what became labelled as the 'anti-psychiatry movement', which won such a high profile in the 1960s and 1970s. Its tenets were varied and controversial: mental illness was not an objective behavioural or biochemical reality but either a negative label or a strategy for coping in a mad world; madness had a truth of its own; and psychosis could be a healing process and, hence, should not be pharmacologically suppressed. What was common to anti-psychiatry, however, was the critique of the asylum. The leading American spokesman Thomas Szasz, as we have seen, exposed *The Myth of Mental Illness* (1961) and *The Manufacture of Madness* (1970), as part of a thoroughgoing critique of 'compulsory psychiatry'—turning patients into prisoners. The Chicago sociologist Erving Goffman meanwhile exposed the evils of 'total institutions' in his *Asylums* (1961). In Italy, leadership was assumed by the psychiatrist Franco Basaglia, who helped engineer the rapid closure of institutions (chaos resulted), while in the Netherlands the glamorous and mystically inclined Jan Foudraine was to the fore in a movement which enlisted the sympathies of students protesting against state and professional power.

In Britain anti-psychiatry's leader was the equally charismatic Ronald Laing (1927–89), a Glaswegian psychiatrist influenced by Sartre's existential philosophy. 'Madness', he wrote in a characteristic aphorism, 'need not be all breakdown. It may also be break-through. It is potential liberation and renewal as well as enslavement and existential death.' In 1965 he established Kingsley Hall, a community ('hospital' was avoided) in a working-class East London neighbourhood where residents and psychiatrists lived under the same roof. The latter were to 'assist' patients in living through the full-scale regression involved in schizophrenia. A brilliant writer, Laing won a cult following at the time of the counter-culture and student protests against the Vietnam War. Films like *Family Life* (1971) and *One Flew Over the Cuckoo's Nest* (1975) meanwhile mobilized opinion against gothic asylums and the policing and normalizing roles of psychiatry.

Mainly associated with left-wing politics, anti-psychiatry thus urged de-institutionalization. At the same time, and from a wholly different angle, politicians of the radical right, including Ronald Reagan in the USA and Margaret Thatcher in the UK, lent their support to 'community care', being hostile to welfarism and keen to cut costly psychiatric beds. As early as 1961 Enoch Powell, the then Conservative British Minister of Health, had announced that the old mental hospitals—'isolated, majestic, imperious, brooded over by the gigantic water tower and chimney combined, rising unmistakable and daunting out of the countryside'—should be closed down or scaled down.

Inmate populations were rapidly reduced—in Britain from around 150,000 in 1950 to just a fifth of that number by the 1980s. Whether community care worked, however, was another matter, and public fears

were voiced about patient welfare—and the danger-
ousness of poorly supervised ex-patients.

By the close of the twentieth century, the psychiatric
hospital and orthodox Freudian psychoanalysis, both
inextricably identified with psychiatry at mid-century,
were equally out of favour and on the wane. The West
had meanwhile seen, however, an explosive growth in
the supposed incidence of a fast-growing profusion of
supposed psychiatric conditions—post traumatic stress
disorder (PTSD) and repressed memory syndrome
being just two amongst dozens. Partly to counter them,
there had also arisen a constellation of psychotherapies
which had transformed the handling of mental problems through techniques involving group sessions, family therapy, consciousness-raising, sensitivity training,
game- and role-playing, and behaviour modification
through stimulus and reinforcement. Clinical psychology and cognitive therapy had been born and
boomed. These days clinics and techniques for psycho-
social problems, sexual dysfunctions, eating disorders,
and personal relations continue to proliferate—while
prospects are held out of a pill for every psychological
ill.

Business as usual

Meantime, mainstream academic and hospital psychiatry remained committed to the programme of describing and taxonomizing the mental disorders stemming from Kraepelin. The *Diagnostic and Statistical Manual* of the American Psychiatric Association—the profession's diagnostic handbook—was first published in 1952. In 1980, a revised version, *DSM-III*, mapped the following broad categories of mental disorder: disorders of childhood or infancy (hyperactivity, anorexia, retardation, autism); known organic cause (disease of old age, drug-induced); disorders of schizophrenia (disorganized, catatonia, paranoid, undifferentiated); paranoid disorders (without schizophrenic signs); affective disorders (bipolar, major depressive); anxiety disorders (phobias, obsessive-compulsive); somatoform (conversion disorder, hypochondriasis); dissociative (fugue states, amnesia, multiple personality); and personality disorders. The publication in 1994 of *DSM-IV* confirmed the trend away from the psychogenic theories dominant in America a generation before, towards a more organic orientation. It also brought a fresh crop of disorder labels. Indeed, a glance at successive editions of the *DSM*, which requires energetic revision every few years, reveals different, and often incompatible or overlapping, terminologies, coming and going from edition to edition. A notorious postal vote, held by the American Psychiatric Association in 1975, led to the belated removal of homosexuality from its slate of afflictions. It is not only cynics who claim that politico-cultural, racial, and gender prejudices still shape the diagnosis of what are purportedly objective disease syndromes. Most telling of all has been the sheer explosion in the enterprise's scale: the first edition was some hundred pages; *DSM-II* ran to 134 pages, *DSM-III* to almost 500; the latest revision, *DSM-IV-TR* (2000) is a staggering 943 pages! More people seem to be diagnosed as suffering from more psychiatric disorders than ever: is that progress?

9

Conclusion: modern times, ancient problems?

This very brief survey hasn't attempted to probe the anthropological or social causes of mental illness—of civilization and its discontents; nor has it sought to show the social functions of madness and psychiatry, or to resolve any number of similarly historically impalpable questions. In a far more focused, down-to-earth way, I have concentrated on a narrative of notions of mental illness, and treatments of the mad, since records began.

As the twentieth century dawned, the *British Medical Journal* sounded an upbeat note: 'in no department of medicine, perhaps, is the contrast between the knowledge and practice in 1800 and the knowledge and practice in 1900 so great as in the department that deals with insanity.' Not so the specialist—and hence more authoritative?—*Journal of Mental Science.* Pointing in the very same year to the 'apparent inefficacy of medicine in the cure of insanity', it seemed depressed:

'though medical science has made great advances during the nineteenth century, our knowledge of the *mental* functions of the brain is still comparatively obscure.' *Lancet* for its part managed to look in both directions at once, claiming in an editorial in 1913 that only then and belatedly was 'British psychiatry beginning to awake from its lethargy'.

At the dawn of the twenty-first century, a similar confusion of tongues may be heard regarding the psychiatric balance sheet. For some, the twentieth century brought Freud's revelation of the true dynamics of the psyche; for others, psychoanalysis proved a sterile interlude, before neurophysiological and neurochemical understanding of the brain finally advanced and bore fruit in effective medications. Psycho-pharmaceutical developments certainly allow psychiatry itself to function better, but pacifying patients with drugs hardly seems the pinnacle of achievement and any claims as to the maturity of a science of mental disorders seem premature and contestable—witness the wholesale comings and goings of disease classifications from *The Diagnostic and Statistical Manual.*

The psychotropics revolution, the patients' rights movement, and the scandal of crumbling asylums fused to launch the 'decarceration' policies favoured since the 1960s. The difficulties that followed are all too familiar. Controversy rages, within and beyond the profession, about the success (or failure) of de-institutionalization and community care, leading to calls (from both the profession and the public) to bring back the traditional asylum as a safe haven for the insane. In such circumstances, psychiatry itself may seem somewhat disoriented. Meanwhile, whether treatment of the mentally ill actually became more humane in a century which gassed tens of thousands of schizophrenics is a question permitting no comforting answers about rationality and sanity.

Once under siege from anti-psychiatry *à la* Laing, the discipline has undoubtedly weathered that storm. But it still lacks the cognitive and professional unity enjoyed by general medicine and remains torn between bio-psychosocial and medical models both of its object and of its therapeutic strategies.

Meanwhile, partly because of the proliferation of psy-chiatries, more people are said to be suffering—indeed *claiming* to be suffering—from a proliferation of psychi-atric syndromes, in a 'victim culture' in which benefits may appear to lie in buying into psychiatric paradigms. More people than ever swallow the medications, and perhaps even the theories, which psychiatry prescribes, and attend various sorts of therapists, as the idioms of the psychological and the psychiatric replace

Christianity and humanism as the ways of making sense of self—to oneself, one's peers, and the authorities. Yet public confidence in the psychiatric profession is low, as is evident from the ubiquitously distrustful images in the arts and reports in the popular press. Is Folly jingling its bells once again?

Further reading

The last generation has brought a vast proliferation of publications in the history of psychiatry. Much is based upon deep analysis of archival materials (for instance, hospital and institutional records). Much is also, explicitly or not, *parti pris* and polemical; and lively—not to say vitriolic—controversies rage in books and scholarly journals, generally between (alleged) supporters and (alleged) opponents of the established psychiatric enterprise. It would not be appropriate in this brief guide to explore such allegiances in any detail. Mark Micale and Roy Porter (eds.), *Discovering the History of Psychiatry* (New York and Oxford: Oxford University Press, 1994) offers extended critical bibliographical and historiographical essays for materials published up to the early 1990s. For evaluation of monographs published since then, consult the reviews section in such periodicals as *History of Psychiatry* and *Journal of the History of the Behavioral Sciences*.

In the following listing, scholarly articles have, on the whole, been omitted for the sake of brevity, and I have also concentrated almost exclusively on English-language material. I have further chosen to omit the enormous recent literature in the fields of literary theory, women's and cultural studies, and body history which deploys Freudian and Lacanian perspectives to explore the construction of the self: it is beyond the scope of this book.

Chapter 1: Introduction
The best, up-to-date, readable history of psychiatry is Edward Shorter's *A History of Psychiatry. From the Era of the Asylum to the Age*

of Prozac (New York: Wiley, 1997). Its historical prejudices are plain to see. Older works include Franz G. Alexander and Sheldon T. Selesnick, *The History of Psychiatry: An Evaluation of Psychiatric Thought and Practice from Prehistoric Times to the Present* (London: George Allen & Unwin, 1967), which is psychoanalytically slanted. Brief is E. H. Ackerknecht, *A Short History of Psychiatry*, 2nd edn, trans. Sula Wolff (New York: Hafner, 1968), and briefer still is William F. Bynum, 'Psychiatry in Its Historical Context', in M. Shepherd and O. L. Zangwill (eds.), *Handbook of Psychiatry*, vol. i : *General Psychopathology* (Cambridge: Cambridge University Press, 1983), 11–38. The history of clinical psychiatry and its concepts is addressed in G. E. Berrios, *History of Mental Symptoms* (Cambridge: Cambridge University Press, 1996) and German Berrios and Roy Porter (eds.), *A History of Clinical Psychiatry. The Origin and History of Psychiatric Disorders* (London: Athlone, 1995).

Various anthologies afford introductions to primary texts. These include John Paul Brady (ed.), *Classics of American Psychiatry: 1810–1934* (St Louis: Warren H. Green, Inc., 1975); Charles E. Goshen, *Documentary History of Psychiatry: A Source Book on Historical Principles* (London: Vision, 1967); Richard Hunter and Ida Macalpine, *Three Hundred Years of Psychiatry: 1535–1860* (London: Oxford University Press, 1963); and Bert Kaplan, *The Inner World of Mental Illness* (New York: Harper & Row, 1964).

Useful works of reference are John Howells (ed.), *World History of Psychiatry* (New York: Bruner/Mazel, 1968); and John G. Howells and M. Livia Osborn, *A Reference Companion to the History of Abnormal Psychology* (Westport, Conn.: Greenwood Press, 1984).

On the question, mooted in this Introduction, of the reality of mental illness, see Thomas S. Szasz, *The Manufacture of Madness*

(New York: Dell, 1970; London: Paladin, 1972); *idem, The Myth of Mental Illness: Foundations of a Theory of Personal Conduct* (rev. edn., New York: Harper & Row, 1974); and *idem, The Age of Madness: The History of Involuntary Mental Hospitalization Presented in Selected Texts* (London: Routledge & Kegan Paul, 1975); see also Michel Foucault, *La Folie et la Déraison: Histoire de la Folie à l'Age Classique* (Paris: Librairie Plon, 1961); abridged as *Madness and Civilization: A History of Insanity in the Age of Reason*, trans. Richard Howard (New York: Random House, 1965)—the most searching analysis of the symbiotic histories of reason and unreason. For critical discussion, see Arthur Still and Irving Velody (eds.), *Rewriting the History of Madness: Studies in Foucault's 'Histoire de la Folie'* (London and New York: Routledge, 1992), and Martin Roth and Jerome Kroll, *The Reality of Mental Illness* (Cambridge: Cambridge University Press, 1986). Klaus Doerner's *Bürger und Irre* (Frankfurt-am-Main: Europäische Verlaganstalt, 1969) English trans.: *Madmen and the Bourgeoisie: A Social History of Insanity and Psychiatry* (Oxford: Basil Blackwell, 1981) follows a similar trail to Foucault.

Recent studies which historically illuminate the question of the reality, persistence, or transience of mental illnesses are Ian Hacking, *Mad Travellers: Reflections on the Reality of Transient Mental Illnesses* (London: Free Association Books, 1999) and Walter Vandereycken and Ron Van Deth, *From Fasting Saints to Anorexic Girls: The History of Self-Starvation* (London: Athlone Press, 1994).

Chapter 2: Gods and demons

For madness and the gods in Greek culture, see Bennett Simon, *Mind and Madness in Ancient Greece* (Ithaca, NY: Cornell University Press, 1978) and Ruth Padel, *In and Out of the Mind:*

Greek Images of the Tragic Self (Princeton: Princeton University Press, 1992). For the supernatural and the psyche in the Middle Ages, consult Penelope E. R. Doob, *Nebuchadnezzar's Children: Conventions of Madness in Middle English Literature* (New Haven and London: Yale University Press, 1974), and Basil Clarke, *Mental Disorder in Earlier Britain* (Cardiff: University of Wales Press, 1975). Particular early modern contexts are examined in Michael MacDonald, *Mystical Bedlam: Madness, Anxiety and Healing in Seventeenth Century England* (Cambridge: Cambridge University Press, 1981); *idem, Witchcraft and Hysteria in Elizabethan London: Edward Jorden and the Mary Glover Case* (London: Routledge, 1991), and H. C. Erik Midelfort, *A History of Madness in Sixteenth Century Germany* (Stanford, Calif.: Stanford University Press, 1997). Gregory Zilboorg's *The Medical Man and the Witch During the Renaissance* (Baltimore: Johns Hopkins University Press, 1935) is provocative but dated.

Far the best account of the rational critique of demonology is Michael Heyd, *'Be Sober and Reasonable', The Critique of Enthusiasm in the Seventeenth and Early Eighteenth Centuries* (Leiden; New York; Köln: E. J. Brill, 1995).

For George Trosse, see *The Life of the Reverend Mr. George Trosse: Written by Himself, and Published posthumously According to His Order in 1714*, ed. A. W. Brink (Montreal: McGill-Queen's University Press, 1974).

Chapter 3: Madness rationalized

The humoralist tradition within which theories of mania and melancholy were situated is explained in James N. Longrigg, *Greek Rational Medicine* (London: Routledge, 1993); E. D. Phillips, *Greek Medicine* (London: Thames & Hudson, 1973); and V. Nutton,

'Humoralism', in W. F. Bynum and Roy Porter (eds.), *Companion Encyclopedia of the History of Medicine* (London: Routledge, 1993), 281–91. For ancient ideas about madness, see G. A. Roccatagliata, *A History of Ancient Psychiatry* (Westport, Conn.: Greenwood Press, 1986). For later developments of such views, S. W. Jackson's *Melancholia and Depression: from Hippocratic Times to Modern Times* (New Haven: Yale University Press, 1986) is excellent.

For the Islamic tradition, consult Michael W. Dols, *Majnūn: The Madman in Medieval Islamic Society* (Oxford: Clarendon Press, 1992); medieval Western ideas are explored in Nancy G. Siraisi, *Medieval and Early Renaissance Medicine: An Introduction to Knowledge and Practice* (Chicago and London: Chicago University Press, 1990). And for Renaissance thinking see Andrew Wear, Roger French, and Iain Lonie (eds.), *The Medical Renaissance of the Sixteenth Century* (Cambridge: Cambridge University Press, 1985).

The best scholarly edition of Robert Burton's *The Anatomy of Melancholy* is that edited by N. K. Kiessling, T. C. Faulkner, and R. L. Blair (Oxford: Oxford University Press, 1990); on Burton see L. Babb, *Sanity in Bedlam: A Study of Robert Burton's Anatomy of Melancholy* (East Lansing, Mich.: Michigan State University Press, 1959) and Berger Evans, *The Psychiatry of Robert Burton* (New York: Octagon Books, 1972).

For the new seventeenth-century turn in psychiatric thinking, see T. Brown, 'Descartes, Dualism and Psychosomatic Medicine', in W. F. Bynum, Roy Porter, and M. Shepherd (eds.), *The Anatomy of Madness*, vol. i (London: Tavistock, 1985), 151–65. Also good on Descartes is R. B. Carter, *Descartes' Medical Philosophy: The Organic Solution to the Mind–Body Problem* (Baltimore: Johns Hopkins University Press, 1983). Interesting on Hobbes is Jeffrey Barnouw, 'Hobbes's Psychology of Thought: Endeavours,

Purpose and Curiosity', *History of European Ideas*, x (1990), 519–45, while for Locke consult John W. Yolton, *John Locke and the Way of Ideas* (Oxford: Oxford University Press, 1956).

Chapter 4: Fools and folly

On madness and stigma see Erving Goffman, *Stigma: Notes on the Management of Spoiled Identity* (Harmondsworth: Penguin, 1970); Sander Gilman, *Difference and Pathology* (Ithaca, NY, and London: Cornell University Press, 1985); and *idem, Disease and Representation. From Madness to AIDS* (Ithaca, NY: Cornell University Press, 1988). For images of the mad—and also for the art of the insane—see Sander L. Gilman, *Seeing the Insane* (New York: Brunner, Mazel, 1982) and J. M. MacGregor, *The Discovery of the Art of the Insane* (Princeton: Princeton University Press, 1989).

A survey of literary renderings of madness is offered by L. Feder, *Madness in Literature* (Princeton: Princeton University Press, 1980); for the early modern period, Robert S. Kinsman, 'Folly, Melancholy and Madness: A Study in Shifting Styles of Medical Analysis and Treatment, 1450–1675', in R. S. Kinsman (ed.), *The Darker Vision of the Renaissance: Beyond the Fields of Reason* (Berkeley: University of California Press, 1974), 273–320, and Duncan Salkeld, *Madness and Drama in the Age of Shakespeare* (Manchester: Manchester University Press 1993) are illuminating. Love folly is the theme of Jacques Ferrand's *A Treatise on Lovesickness*, trans. and ed. D. A. Beecher and M. Ciavolella (Syracuse, NY: Syracuse University Press, 1990), which is evaluated in M. F. Wack, *Lovesickness in the Middle Ages: The Viaticum and its Commentaries* (Philadelphia: University of Pennsylvania Press, 1990). Later literature/madness interfaces are probed in Allan Ingram's *The Madhouse of Language: Writing and Reading Madness in the Eighteenth Century* (London/New York: Routledge, 1991), Max Byrd's *Visits to Bedlam: Madness and Literature in the Eighteenth Century* (Columbia: University of South Carolina Press, 1974), and Michael V. DePorte's *Nightmares and Hobby Horses: Swift, Sterne, and Augustan Ideas of Madness* (San Marino, Calif.: Huntingdon Library, 1974).

The question of fashionable diseases underpins the account of hysteria in Sander L. Gilman, Helen King, Roy Porter, G. S. Rousseau, and Elaine Showalter, *Hysteria Beyond Freud* (Berkeley, Los Angeles, and London: University of California Press, 1993). Cheyne's book is reproduced as *The English Malady; or, A Treatise of Nervous Diseases of all Kinds, with the Author's Own Case* (London: G. Strahan, 1733; repr. edn., ed. Roy Porter, Routledge, 1991).

The madness and genius debate is further debated in G. Becker, *The Mad Genius Controversy* (London and Beverly Hills: Sage, 1978). For degenerationism, see Daniel Pick, *Faces of Degeneration: A European Disorder, c.1848–1918* (Cambridge: Cambridge University Press, 1989) and Tony James's *Dream, Creativity and Madness in Nineteenth Century France* (Oxford: Clarendon Press, 1995); and for today's discussions, see Kay Redfield Jamison's *Touched with Fire: Manic-Depressive Illness and the Artistic Temperament* (New York: Free Press, 1993), Oliver Sacks's *A Leg to Stand On* (London: Duckworth, 1984), Louis A. Sass's *Madness and Modernism: Insanity in the Light of Modern Art, Literature and Thought* (New York: Basic Books, 1994), and George Pickering's *Creative Malady*, (London: George Allen & Unwin, 1974).

The growing centrality of women to psychiatry over the last couple of centuries is superbly handled in Elaine Showalter's *The Female Malady: Women, Madness, and English Culture, 1830–1980* (New York: Pantheon Press, 1986)—Yannick Ripa, *Women and*

Madness: The Incarceration of Women in Nineteenth Century France, trans. Catherine Menage (Cambridge: Polity Press in Association with Basil Blackwell, 1990) is good for France.

Chapter 5: Locking up the mad
For a brief survey, with extensive references, of institutionalization, see Roy Porter, 'Madness and its Institutions', in Andrew Wear (ed.), *Medicine in Society* (Cambridge: Cambridge University Press, 1992), 277–301. The key analyses are Foucault (see above) and Andrew Scull, *Museums of Madness: The Social Organization of Insanity in Nineteenth-Century England* (London: Allen Lane, 1979)—this has appeared in revised form as *The Most Solitary of Afflictions: Madness and Society in Britain, 1700–1900* (New Haven and London: Yale University Press, 1993). For the USA, consult David Rothman, *The Discovery of the Asylum: Social Order and Disorder in the New Republic* (Boston: Little, Brown, 1971) and Gerald Grob, *The Mad Among Us: A History of the Care of America's Mentally Ill* (New York: Free Press, 1994); and for France, Robert Castel, *L'Ordre Psychiatrique: L'Age d'Or d'Aliénisme* (Paris: Maspéro, 1973; Paris: Editions de Minuit, 1976); English trans. W. D. Halls, *The Regulation of Madness: Origins of Incarceration in France* (Berkeley: University of California Press; Cambridge: Polity Press, 1988); and Françoise and Robert Castel and Anne Lovell, *The Psychiatric Society* (New York: Columbia University Press, 1981).

A pioneering account of one distinctively English sector was William Llewellyn Parry-Jones, *The Trade in Lunacy: A Study of Private Madhouses in England in the Eighteenth and Nineteenth Centuries* (London: Routledge & Kegan Paul, 1971). A recent study of the oldest institution of all is Jonathan Andrews, Asa Briggs, Roy Porter, Penny Tucker, and Keir Waddington, *The History of Bethlem*

(London: Routledge, 1997), while mad-doctoring is explored in Andrew Scull, Charlotte MacKenzie and Nicholas Hervey, *Masters of Bedlam: The Transformation of the Mad-Doctoring Trade* (Princeton: Princeton University Press, 1996).

'Moral treatment' and 'moral therapy' form the core of Anne Digby, *Madness, Morality and Medicine: A Study of the York Retreat, 1796–1914* (Cambridge: Cambridge University Press, 1985). George III's case is expertly analysed in Ida Macalpine and Richard Hunter, *George III and the Mad Business* (London: Allen Lane, 1969). Institutional psychiatry for rich and the poor can be contrasted through Charlotte MacKenzie's *Psychiatry for the Rich: A History of Ticehurst Private Asylum, 1792–1917* (London and New York: Routledge, 1993) and Richard Hunter and Ida Macalpine's *Psychiatry for the Poor, 1851. Colney Hatch Asylum, Friern Hospital 1973: A Medical and Social History* (London: Dawsons, 1974). The 'myth' of Pinel is exploded in Dora B. Weiner, ' "*Le Geste de Pinel*": The History of a Psychiatric Myth', in Mark Micale and Roy Porter (eds.), *Discovering the History of Psychiatry* (New York and Oxford: Oxford University Press, 1994), 343–470.

For today's more nuanced accounts of the complex forces behind institutionalization, the following are illuminating: Peter Bartlett, *The Poor Law of Lunacy: Administration of Pauper Lunatics in Nineteenth-Century England* (London: Cassell Academic, 1998); Peter Bartlett and David Wright (eds.), *Outside the Walls of the Asylum: The History of Care in the Community 1750–2000* (London and New Brunswick, NJ: Athlone Press, 1999); Leonard D. Smith, *Cure, Comfort and Safe Custody: Public Lunatic Asylums in Early Nineteenth-Century England* (London: Cassell, 1999); and Joseph Melling and Bill Forsythe (eds.), *Insanity, Institutions and Society: New Research in the Social History of Madness, 1800–1914* (London:

Routledge, 1999). World perspectives on institutionalization are offered in Roy Porter and David Wright (eds.), *The Confinement of the Insane in the Modern Era: International Perspectives* (Cambridge: Cambridge University Press, forthcoming).

Chapter 6: The rise of psychiatry

Enlightenment orientations of British psychiatry are explained in Roy Porter, *Mind Forg'd Manacles: Madness and Psychiatry in England from Restoration to Regency* (London: Athlone Press, 1987; paperback edn., Penguin, 1990) and Akihito Suzuki, 'An Anti-Lockean Enlightenment?: Mind and Body in Early Eighteenth-Century English Medicine', in Roy Porter (ed.), *Medicine and the Enlightenment* (Amsterdam: Rodopi, 1994), 226–59. The roles of Pinel, Esquirol, and the tradition leading to Charcot are penetratingly discussed in Jan Goldstein, *Console and Classify: The French Psychiatric Profession in the Nineteenth Century* (Cambridge: Cambridge University Press, 1987).

Nineteenth-century German psychiatry is clarified in numerous writings by Otto Marx: 'German Romantic Psychiatry: Part 1', *History of Psychiatry*, i (1990), 351–80; *idem*, 'German Romantic Psychiatry: Part 2', *History of Psychiatry*, ii (1991), 1–26; *idem*, 'Nineteenth Century Medical Psychology: Theoretical Problems in the Work of Griesinger, Meynert, and Wernicke', *Isis*, 61 (1970), 355–70; *idem*, 'Wilhelm Griesinger and the History of Psychiatry: A Reassessment', *Bulletin of the History of Medicine*, 46 (1972), 519–44. For neurasthenia, consult Janet Oppenheim, *'Shattered Nerves': Doctors, Patients and Depression in Victorian England* (Oxford: Oxford University Press, 1991) and Marijke Gijswijt-Hofstra and Roy Porter (eds.), *Cultures of Neurasthenia: From Beard to the First World War* (Amsterdam: Rodopi, 2001).

For the specialty of forensic psychiatry, most illuminating are Roger Smith's *Trial by Medicine: Insanity and Responsibility in Victorian Trials* (Edinburgh: Edinburgh University Press, 1981) and Joel Peter Eigen's *Witnessing Insanity: Madness and Mad-Doctors in the English Court* (New Haven: Yale University Press, 1995); a comprehensive but flawed survey is Daniel N. Robinson's *Wild Beasts and Idle Humours: The Insanity Defense from Antiquity to the Present* (Cambridge, Mass.: Harvard University Press, 1995).

Extracts from nineteenth-century English psychiatric texts may be found in Vieda Skultans, *Madness and Morals: Ideas on Insanity in the Nineteenth Century* (London and Boston: Routledge & Kegan Paul, 1975).

Chapter 7: The mad

Autobiographical writings of 'mad' people have been anthologized and surveyed in Dale Peterson (ed.), *A Mad People's History of Madness* (Pittsburgh: University of Pittsburgh Press, 1982); Michael Glenn (ed.), *Voices from the Asylum* (New York: Harper & Row, 1974); Allan Ingram, *Voices of Madness: Four Pamphlets, 1683–1796* (Stroud: Sutton Publishing, 1997) and Roy Porter (ed.), *The Faber Book of Madness* (London: Faber, 1991; paperback 1993). Some attempt at reproducing their 'view' is offered in Roy Porter, *A Social History of Madness: Stories of the Insane* (London: Weidenfeld & Nicolson, 1987).

Specifically for Margery Kempe, see *The Book of Margery Kempe* (Harmondsworth: Penguin, 1985)—for an attempt to understand her against the background of the religious beliefs of the time, see P. R. Freeman *et al.*, 'Margery Kempe, a New Theory: the Inadequacy of Hysteria and Postpartum Psychosis as Diagnostic Categories', *History of Psychiatry*, i (1990), 169–90. For John

Perceval see J. T. Perceval, *A Narrative of the Treatment Received by a Gentleman, During a State of Mental Derangement* (London: Effingham Wilson, 1838). For Clifford Beers, see Clifford Beers, *A Mind That Found Itself: An Autobiography* (Pittsburgh: University of Pittsburgh Press, 1981) and Norman Dain, *Clifford W. Beers: Advocate for the Insane* (Pittsburgh: University of Pittsburgh Press, 1980); and for James Tilley Matthews see John Haslam, *Illustrations of Madness* (London: Rivingtons, printed by G. Hayden, 1810); ed. Roy Porter (London: Routledge, 1988).

Chapter 8: The century of psychoanalysis?

On Kraepelin and his tradition, see German Berrios and Renate Hauser, 'Kraepelin', in German E. Berrios and Roy Porter (eds.), *A History of Clinical Psychiatry: The Origin and History of Psychiatric Disorders* (London: Athlone, 1995), 280–91 and E. Engstrom, 'Institutional Aspects in the Development of Emil Kraepelin's Nosology', in ibid. 292–301. Relevant too is G. E. Berrios and H. L. Freeman (eds.), *Alzheimer and the Dementias* (London: Royal Society of Medicine Services Limited, 1992). For Nazi psychiatry, see Geoffrey Cocks, *Psychotherapy in the Third Reich: The Göring Institute* (New York: Oxford University Press, 1985).

Freud studies are now so extensive and intricate as to defy summary. The best sympathetic biography remains Peter Gay's *Freud: A Life for Our Time* (London: Dent, 1988); the most iconoclastic account is Jeffrey M. Masson's *The Assault on Truth: Freud's Suppression of the Seduction Theory* (New York: Farrar, Straus & Giroux, 1983). Some approaches to Freud are canvassed in John Forrester, ' "A Whole Climate of Opinion": Rewriting the History of Psychoanalysis', in Mark Micale and Roy Porter (eds.), *Discovering the History of Psychiatry* (New York and Oxford: Oxford

University Press, 1994), 174–90; Forrester assesses the modern Freudian debate in *Dispatches from the Freud Wars: Psychoanalysis and its Passions* (Cambridge, Mass.: Harvard University Press, 1997). The wider question of the unconscious is handled in a masterly way in Henri F. Ellenberger's *The Discovery of the Unconscious: The History and Evolution of Dynamic Psychiatry* (New York: Basic Books, 1970); while essential background for understanding Freud is to be found in Mark Micale, *Approaching Hysteria: Disease and its Representations* (Princeton: Princeton University Press, 1994). For the psychoanalytical movement, see Joseph Schwartz, *Cassandra's Daughter: A History of Psychoanalysis in Europe and America* (London: Allen Lane, 1999), and specifically for Jung, see John Kerr, *A Most Dangerous Method* (London: Sinclair Stevenson, 1993) and Frank McLynn, *Carl Gustav Jung* (London: Bantam Press, 1996).

Twentieth-century therapeutics form the subject of Elliot S. Valenstein's *Great and Desperate Cures: The Rise and Decline of Psychosurgery and Other Radical Treatments for Mental Illness* (New York: Basic Books, 1986), and Jack Pressman's *Last Resort: Psychosurgery and the Limits of Medicine* (Cambridge: Cambridge University Press, 1998).

For the attack on the asylum, see Andrew Scull, *Decarceration: Community Treatment and the Deviant—A Radical View*, 2nd edn. (Oxford: Polity Press; New Brunswick, NJ: Rutgers University Press, 1984); see also Peter Barham, *From the Mental Patient to the Person* (London: Routledge, 1991), and *idem, Closing the Asylum: The Mental Patient in Modern Society* (Harmondsworth: Penguin Books, 1992).

Many aspects of the British story are covered in German Berrios and Hugh Freeman (eds.), *150 Years of British Psychiatry,*

1841–1991 (London: Gaskell, 1991) and Hugh Freeman and German Berrios (eds.), *150 Years of British Psychiatry*, vol. ii: *The Aftermath* (London and Atlantic Highlands, NJ: Athlone, 1996).

There is now a large literature on shell shock and the ubiquitous theory of 'trauma' which has emerged from it. See Edward M. Brown, 'Creating Traumatic Emotional Disorders Before and During World War I', in German Berrios and Roy Porter (eds.), *A History of Clinical Psychiatry: The Origin and History of Psychiatric Disorders* (London: Athlone, 1995), 501–8, Harold Merskey, 'Shell Shock', in German Berrios and Hugh Freeman (eds.), *150 Years of British Psychiatry, 1841–1991* (London: Gaskell, 1991), 245–67, Ben Shepherd, *A War of Nerves: Soldiers and Psychiatrists 1914–1994* (London: Cape, 2001), and, most recently, the wide-ranging work ed. Mark Micale and Paul Lerner, *Traumatic Pasts: Histories, Psychiatry and Trauma in the Modern Age, 1870–1930* (Cambridge: Cambridge University Press, 2001). Depression and related conditions are covered in Edward Shorter, *From Paralysis to Fatigue. A History of Psychosomatic Illness in the Modern Era* (New York: Free Press, 1992); *idem, From the Mind into the Body: The Cultural Origins of Psychosomatic Symptoms* (New York: Free Press, 1994), and Andrew Solomon, *The Noonday Demon: An Atlas of Depression* (London: Chatto & Windus, 2001).

For the psychopharmacological revolution, see David Healy, *The Antidepressant Era* (Cambridge, Mass.: Harvard University Press, 1997) and Peter D. Kramer, *Listening to Prozac* (London: Fourth Estate, 1994). Sargant's prediction is in *The Unquiet Mind. The Autobiography of a Physician in Psychological Medicine* (London: Heinemann, 1967).

The entertaining tale of *DSM* is told in H. Kutchins and S. A. Kirk, *Making Us Crazy: The Psychiatric Bible and the Creation of Mental Disorders* (New York: Free Press, 1997).

Index

Numbers in *italic* indicate illustrations